HOW TO OVERCOME FAILURE & MASTER SUCCESS
IN YOUR HEALTH, WEALTH, AND RELATIONSHIPS

FROM BROKEN
TO BOLD

LARA TUGBIYELE

FROM BROKEN TO BOLD
How To Overcome Failure & Master Success in Your Health,
Wealth, and Relationships

Book Design by
Transcendent Publishing

Editing by Mary Rembert

ISBN: 979-8-9900956-3-2

Unless otherwise noted, all scripture verses are from the New King James Version (NKJV).

Printed in the United States of America.

DEDICATION

"… to give them beauty for ashes, the oil of joy for mourning, the garment of praise instead for the spirit of heaviness …" (Isaiah 61:3).

It is with absolute great joy that I dedicate this book to my Abba Father. Lord, you have my yes! Thank you for believing in me …

In heartfelt dedication to my confidant and the love that colors every chapter of my life. To my husband, whose support and presence have been the inspiration behind every word written on these pages. You are the enduring melody that resonates through the narrative of our journey together.

Finally, to our three wonderful children, Hazel, Hadassa, and Joshua. May you never limit the power of God in your life. Now, go and transform the world!

TABLE OF CONTENTS

INTRODUCTION

I'm thrilled that you've chosen to pick up a copy of this book and explore its contents. I want to emphasize that within these pages, you won't find untested theories; instead, you'll discover strategies that I have personally used to transition from a state of failure and despair to a place of victory and success in all aspects of my life, including my finances, relationships, and health.

I'd like to share my story to inspire and perhaps challenge you. I was born in Nigeria, West Africa, and from the moment my mother became pregnant with me, I faced rejection from my father simply because I was a girl. He already had one daughter and didn't want another. As I grew up, my father's disdain for me and my younger sister was palpable. We were part of a family of six children struggling in extreme poverty. I know what it's like to go hungry. There were times when we eagerly waited for my father to finish his meal so that we could have his leftovers, even sucking on the scraps of his chicken bones.

I grew up witnessing my father's cruelty toward my mother. He was an intensely angry man, subjecting us to relentless physical, verbal, and emotional abuse. He frequently called me "stupid" and made sure to remind me constantly that I would never amount to anything in life. Eventually, my mom made the courageous decision to leave Nigeria and move to America, where she worked tirelessly for seven years to save enough money to come back and rescue us from our abusive father.

During those long seven years, my siblings and I endured immense hardship, living with our father without the presence of our mom. It was an incredibly challenging period filled with all forms of abuse.

Growing up in this kind of environment was nothing short of a nightmare. It was toxic and profoundly dysfunctional. Demonic activities seemed to surround us constantly. Curses, witchcraft, and voodoo were pervasive in our lives. My father's hatred for me was so intense that he couldn't even bear to be in my presence. It was truly a dreadful situation.

By default, I was effectively programmed to fail. Every endeavor I embarked on failed because of my deeply ingrained "failure mindset." The environment I grew up in was a recipe for disaster, chaos, and unrelenting failure.

I often felt like I was under a curse, and perhaps I was. I bear physical marks on my body from a visit to a "voodoo witch doctor" who inscribed them on my chest for so-called "protection." It's quite a surreal experience to reflect on. This is just a brief glimpse into the hardships we endured. The fact that I'm alive and well today, in my right mind, is nothing short of a miracle.

Seven years later, we escaped under the cover of night and made our way to America. However, our challenges didn't end there. Even after relocating to the U.S., my mother and all six of us children found ourselves in a cramped, mouse-infested three-bedroom, one-bathroom apartment in one of the most troubled housing projects in Brooklyn, New York, for another grueling seven years. The struggle was undeniably real, and it felt like I had transitioned from the proverbial "frying pan into the fire," as they say in Africa—going from bad to worse.

During this time, no one had faith in me, and I had lost faith in myself. I continued to operate under the weight of my "failed" programming. Being in school was a constant struggle, until one day ... (the details of this part of the story will be revealed in my next book).

Gradually, the Lord started to impart invaluable lessons to me, teaching me the power of forgiveness, the means to break free from those curses, and the path to renew my mind and find true freedom. Along the way, I was fortunate to have several mentors and coaches who played a crucial role in helping me reprogram my mindset for victory and success.

Today, I can proudly say that I have achieved significant success in every facet of my life—from my business endeavors to my marriage and relationships.

It's important for me to emphasize that I've wholeheartedly forgiven my parents, particularly my father. Although he asked for my forgiveness about a year ago, I had already forgiven him many years before. I recognize that my mother did her best, given the circumstances and her knowledge at the time. I consciously chose to embrace and walk in complete forgiveness as a means to find wholeness.

My experiences growing up have played a pivotal role in shaping the person I've become today. The rejection I faced from my father held a profound value. It led me to seek the face of God as my heavenly Father, and it became the catalyst for my spiritual journey.

The fact that I was severely abused has value. I have marks on my body to remind me of where I started. Even my struggles in school have value. All of my experiences have value. I genuinely believe that all my challenging experiences hold more value than my positive ones because they compelled me to evolve into a warrior. These experiences were instrumental in helping me recognize the inherent potential placed within me by my heavenly Father.

It made me realize that I was designed to prosper and to have dominion, refusing to let my circumstances dictate my future.

In the Bible, the story of Joseph is a remarkable one. He endured numerous trials and suffering, including being sold into slavery by his brothers and unjustly imprisoned for a crime he didn't commit. After many years of hardship, Joseph named his firstborn son Manasseh, which means "God has made me forget all my afflictions," and his second son Ephraim, which means "God has caused me to prosper and be fruitful in the land of my affliction."

Joseph realized that the terrible experiences he endured ultimately became the best things that ever happened to him. In other words, these events happened for him, propelling him into greatness.

I, too, drew inspiration from Joseph's story. I made the deliberate choice to let go of the memories of my afflictions so that I could become the woman God designed me to be and fulfill the destiny He had in store for me. This, in turn, allowed me to have success in all aspects of my life.

Despite the success I now enjoy, I am well aware of what it's like to struggle with poverty, anger, brokenness, and the weight of a failure mindset. This is not a book authored by someone who had life handed to them on a silver platter. Quite the opposite, it's a book written by a person much like you who has faced a challenging life and its share of obstacles.

However, I've managed to find a way to overcome those challenges and achieve success in every facet of my life. I don't take where I am in life for granted. My success is entirely because of the Grace of God.

The strategies I've outlined in this book are not mere theories; they are tried-and-tested approaches that have yielded breakthrough results in my own life.

I am incredibly grateful for God's deliverance, which rescued me from a life that was initially programmed and broken by man's negative words but completely redeemed by the transformative power of God's Word into something far more powerful and promising. He made something beautiful out of my life. And He wants to do the same for you!

CAUGHT UP IN THE WHIRLWIND OF A LACK MINDSET

"Bring my soul out of prison, That I may praise Your name; The righteous shall surround me, For You shall deal bountifully with me."

—Psalm 142:7

This book represents a segment of my story, specifically the portion I wish to share with you at this moment. Why? Because it will encourage you and put the right tools in your hands. Tools you need to win any warfare that may come your way.

I went to college to study Physical Therapy and married shortly after graduating. I loved working with the tiny babies and often told people I had the best job ever.

After I had our daughter, I decided to stay home and home-school her because the Lord told me to. I kicked, screamed, and cried my eyes out because I did not want to be known as a "stay-at-home" mom, which was uncommon back then. After much kicking and screaming, plus the fact that I fear God, I obeyed and stayed home. Let me be honest: I did not like it initially, but God promised I would get my job back when I was ready to go back to work.

Fast forward. Ten years and two more kids later, I decided to return to work as an independent contractor, working only on Fridays. God totally came through with His promise and gave me my job back as He had promised ten years earlier.

I started working once a week, providing PT services to kids in a home care setting. Shortly after, I realized I was severely allergic to cats and needed a strategy each time I went into a particular home. A friend introduced me to essential oils, which I began using. It was very effective for my allergies, watery eyes, sneezing, and all the other things related to allergies. My favorites were combining essential oils like Eucalyptus Radiata, Ravintsara, Myrtle, Peppermint, and Copaiba.

I fell in love with the oils so much that I dove headlong into learning all about them and why they work so well. It fit right into my natural lifestyle. I embraced every bit of it. I decided to join the network marketing company because once I believe in something, I put all my effort into it. I worked my tail off teaching people about essential oils and traveling across the country to teach classes to my team members. I wanted to succeed in this new business venture.

I was introduced to doing vendor events at different places. If you are not familiar with this—you pay for a space, set up your table, and display your products, hoping people will stop and give you eye contact so you can start a conversation with them. I practiced this skill until I became really good at it. Nah, you don't understand. I mean, really, really good at selling. I was known as the "Vendor Event guru." I got our kids involved; sometimes, the whole family traveled with me.

While I'm at it, I might as well let you in on this truth. I love a good challenge, and I am not a quitter.

I was determined to win at this. What was my goal? Hmmm … Good question. I wanted to rank up to the next level in the company.

You see, my childhood was marked by significant trauma. During my mother's pregnancy with me, she endured extensive abuse and rejection from my father. She recounted to me that on the day of my birth, while she was in labor, she had to drive herself to the hospital because my father refused to be involved. This cycle of rejection began before I was even born. As I grew older, my father's animosity toward me intensified, primarily because of my gender. This deep-seated hatred compounded the feelings of rejection I struggled with for an extended period, resulting in a profound identity crisis. To put it bluntly, I was BROKEN!

One of the main problems of having an identity crisis was not knowing who I was. Not knowing who I belonged to because my father rejected me from a very young age. One characteristic of someone with an identity crisis is thinking, "There are never enough resources for them." I kept thinking things would run out, and there wouldn't be enough left for me. This poverty mindset drove me to sign up for so many events at a time. I didn't want to run out of events. I wanted to make sure I always had an event to do.

Most of our weekends looked like this: get up as early as 6 a.m., and load the car with a table, chairs, rugs, bins, bins, and more bins full of oils, freebies, diffusers, and kits. We had everything you could think of in my car. Sometimes, we drove four to five hours from one state to the other so that I could be the one doing these events. I did not realize what was driving me to do them at the time. I thought I just wanted to get to the next level.

I initially believed my goal was simply to advance within the company. Little did I realize, God was preparing to guide me through one of the most profound challenges I would ever face. This trial ultimately resulted in triumph, revealing the depth of God's character and leading me to discover my true identity.

DREAMS, VISIONS, AND PROPHESY

"And it shall come to pass afterward That I will pour out My Spirit on all flesh; Your sons and your daughters shall prophesy, Your old men shall dream dreams, Your young men shall see visions."

—Joel 2:28

On December 29, 2016, I dreamed that I was riding a tricycle really fast, trying to get to the finish line ahead of the others in the race. People to the right cheered us on. A lady beside me was riding her tricycle as fiercely as I was. We looked at each other and locked eyes as if to say, "You can't catch me." But she rode right past me and over the finish line.

I, on the other hand, did not make it to the finish line. Instead, I veered off track toward the left side into the dark area. While in this dark place, I saw a man. "Excuse me," I said. "How can I get to the finish line?"

As He was about to give me directions, I said, "Never mind, I know how to get there." I drove away on my tricycle and ended up right back where I started.

I was very upset in the dream, and then I woke up. You can imagine my reaction to the dream. I was perplexed and wondered what it meant. Exactly seven months later, I had the same exact dream again. This time around, I pondered a bit. I prayed about it, and then I got so "busy" that I left it alone.

Big MISTAKE! The Bible says in Genesis 41:32, "And the dream was repeated to Pharaoh twice because the thing is established by God, and God will shortly bring it to pass." This dream was certainly established by God, and it came to pass.

I wish I could tell you that at that time, I knew exactly how it would pan out! But no. I had no clue. A few months later, I was scrolling on Facebook, and suddenly, a LIVE video of a woman popped up on my feed. Note that I did not know this woman, and I was not friends with her. I quickly clicked on it for some reason. I was interested in what she was talking about. She was rejoicing about her new rank and celebrating with her team members. As I watched closely, this lady was jumping for joy and rejoicing. "Oh my word, this is the same lady riding the tricycle in the dream I had a few months ago!" I exclaimed.

I was shaken! What in the world?! How did she appear on my FB feed? Why? So she went LIVE to announce that she had reached the highest rank in the company. As I watched, I had a flashback to my dream and said aloud, "Wait. This is similar to what happened in my dream. She made it to the finish line." You can only imagine the horror on my face. I was perplexed, confused, and shocked, all at the same time. I had never seen her before in real life.

As I tuned in, a sense of excitement washed over me, bringing back memories of that dream—the tricycle dream from December 2016, which had repeated about seven months later in July 2017. In that dream, the woman rode her tricycle to the finish line while people cheered her on. The very same woman from my dream was now live on my FB feed, celebrating her "ride to the finish line"!

This whole situation struck me as incredibly odd, but because I'm kingdom-minded, I couldn't help but feel that the Lord was speaking to me and teaching me something profound.

Fast forward to April of 2018. I had accidentally signed up for two vendor events on the same day.

A lady who had enrolled with me months prior asked if she could attend one of the events. It was very clear that I could only be in one place at a time. So, I gladly gave her the okay to set up her booth at this venue for free. I had already decided to travel out of the state for the other event. The event I let go of was in the same state I lived in at the time. It was going to be smaller than the one I was planning to attend in D.C. I was also trying to help because she had told me she was interested in building a business, so I figured this was a way to help her get her feet wet. She was so happy to do this event, and so was I. I emailed her all the information the venue coordinator sent me, and that was it. I went and did my event, and she set up and did her own event. Both events were successful. But were they?

She called me at the end of the day to let me know that an incident happened while she was doing her event. A woman had slipped on the mat that she laid on the floor of her booth. According to what she told me during the call, "The woman was on her phone and slipped and fell on her face. She got up from the floor and said she was okay. She admitted that she was looking at her phone and hadn't realized a mat was on the floor." According to her report, several ambulance chasers convinced her to call the ambulance even though she said she was okay. So she did, and they took her to the hospital.

Months went by, and I never once thought about that event or the incident until I got a knock on my door one April afternoon. To my surprise, an older Caucasian gentleman wearing a long black coat was at my door. He began asking questions about the incident. To be honest, I had forgotten all about it, so he had to jog my memory with all the manipulative questions he was asking me.

A few minutes into the conversation with this man, I thought, "I shouldn't be talking to this strange man ... I better stop answering his questions right now." I politely said, "Sir, I'm sorry, but I don't understand what you are saying. I'm in the middle of cooking, and I need to go back to it. Have a good one." I shut the door and slowly backed away. I was irritated and mad that some stranger would dare come to my house to interrogate me like that.

NO WEAPON FORMED ...
SHALL PROSPER

*"No weapon formed against you shall prosper,
And every tongue which rises against you in judgment
You shall condemn."*

—Isaiah 54:17

On a sunny Friday afternoon in June, we decided to sell our house and begin the journey of moving to a different state. We had lived in Pennsylvania for almost 12 years, so moving to a warmer state was very exciting for us. We were at the beginning stages of putting our house on the market. I started purging a little and sold some things on FB marketplace and elsewhere.

But on this particular day, I invited my sister-in-law to stop by my house in the early afternoon to pick up some children's books we no longer needed. About 30 minutes before she arrived, I noticed the garage door had been left open, and a blackbird was inside the garage.

At first, I didn't think anything of it. I pressed the garage button to raise the door up and down, thinking it would trigger the bird to fly out. Nope, the bird did not budge! Instead, it pretended like it was blind or something. I began to wonder what kind of a stupid bird this was.

"Get out of my garage!" I yelled out loud and made noises with a stick I found in the garage. The bird flew right on my car and kept staring at me. I was stunned at the nerve.

I shut the door and went right back inside. Later, my sister-in-law showed up at the house to pick up the books and a few other toys. I jokingly told her not to go out through the garage because a "demonic" bird was in there. We both laughed and didn't think much about it. Time passed, and I told her we needed to start getting ready for my daughter's dance recital, so she decided to head home.

She forgot about my warning not to go out through the garage door, so after grabbing her kids, she opened it. Of course, I yelled from the family room, "Shut the door! I don't want that bird to come inside my house!" But it was too late. She tried to shut the door, but the bird flew past her head and straight into the family room, where it flew all around the high ceiling, making weird noises. The kids (my nephews) were scared and started crying. It turned chaotic fast.

A spirit of confusion literally came inside the room. None of us knew what to do about the bird. A few minutes passed, and I began to sense there was more to this. The bird began to make screeching noises and continued to fly all over the family room. My nephews were traumatized at this point, so I asked my son to take them to the playroom and stay with them until we could get rid of the bird. I began praying in my heavenly language even though I wasn't quite sure what was going on. The bird made its way upstairs and eventually into my daughter's room.

Now, I was furious. I walked up the stairs and told everyone the bird was sent to monitor and wreak havoc, and we must get rid of it fast. I had chills all over my body because I was finally aware of the demonic assignment sent against me.

I began praying and asking God for wisdom. He told us to go into the room where the bird was, and I went in with my daughter and sister-in-law. I did not want this bird to die in my daughter's room. I told everyone to stop throwing things at the bird. I just wanted it out of my house. So my sister-in-law suggested we open the window and the screen. We stopped all our attempts to get rid of the bird, and I prayed silently. Eventually, the bird flew out of my daughter's room.

Phew!

Then, my sister-in-law packed up her kids and left. We had only an hour before my daughter's dance recital, so we quickly freshened up and got ready. I had only 30 minutes to spare to do my daughter's hair. If you are a dance mom, you know exactly what I mean. As we were rushing to leave the house for the dance recital, the doorbell rang.

What in the world?! I was not expecting anyone. I looked through my glass door and recognized the man with the long black coat. My heart sank. I did not answer the door, and he eventually walked away to his car but stayed there in front of my house.

I ran upstairs to my daughter's bedroom and asked the Holy Spirit what to do. He said, "Do you remember what you read in your Bible this morning?" He immediately brought to my mind 2 Chronicles 20:12-17, which I read earlier that morning. He said, "Pay attention to verse 16 first and then verse 17. "Tomorrow, go down against them. They will surely come up by the Ascent of Ziz, and you will find them at the end of the brook before the Wilderness of Jeruel." Verse 17 says: "'You will not *need* to fight in this *battle*. Position yourselves, stand still, and see the salvation of the LORD, who is with you, O Judah and Jerusalem!' Do not fear or be dismayed; tomorrow go out against them, for the LORD is with you."

Taking a cue from verse 16, I understood that the Lord was urging me to summon the courage to head downstairs and confront the situation without directly engaging with this individual. I descended the stairs, gathered the kids, and ushered them into the car. With determination, I opened the garage door and sped out like a maniac, even to the point where the bumper of my car collided with the rising garage door.

What a challenging situation it was. We just managed to make it in time for my daughter's recital. After dropping my kids off at the venue with instructions to save some seats, I searched for a parking spot. Once I parked my car, I started walking toward the venue.

However, as I was crossing a busy street, the strap on my shoe suddenly snapped in the middle of the road. I stumbled and fell right in the midst of traffic. In a panic, I scrambled to my feet because a car was headed straight toward me. Thankfully, the driver narrowly missed me. Surprisingly, no one offered to help, but one lady did ask if I was okay. Before I could muster the courage to respond, she walked away.

Holding back tears, I reached for my phone to call my husband and asked him to meet me at the venue so I could go home while he stayed with the kids. Fortunately, he was only a few minutes away.

I drove home to change my shoes, and my anger was directed toward the devil during the ride home. I began to pray fervently, binding what I perceived as a demonic assault on me.

Upon arriving home, I received clear instructions from the Holy Spirit not to pull into the garage, so I left my car in the driveway. I hurried inside the house to change my shoes. I spent about ten minutes walking around the house, praying in my heavenly language, and pleading for the protective power of the blood of Jesus over our home and the rest of our property.

Once I finished praying, I came out of the house, walked through the garage, and returned to my car. While sitting in my car, I attempted to close the garage door using the remote control. To my frustration, it didn't respond. After several unsuccessful attempts, I stepped out of the car to investigate the issue and noticed that the garage door was completely out of alignment.

I sighed. "Oh boy! Devil, you're really up to some foolish tricks today," I couldn't help but blurt out in frustration. I was feeling quite exasperated, to say the least. I found myself at home, grappling with the challenge of closing my garage door so that I could make it to my daughter's recital on time. Determined, I did the best I could with the situation. I manually pulled the heavy garage door down as far as I could manage. Unfortunately, by the time I arrived at the recital, I had missed one of my daughter's performances. However, I did manage to make it in time to see her second one.

That day weighed heavily on me. It felt like someone had intruded into my home and taken something precious from me. The whole house had an actual foul odor, which was unbearable. I cried myself to sleep that night, overwhelmed by distress.

Let me explain what was happening on this particular day: The bird in question was believed to be a monitoring spirit sent by someone from the law firm to spy on my home. They were eager to gather information about the incident that had occurred back in April with the lady who fell at the vendor event. I hadn't shared any information with them, so they resorted to sending this supposed spirit in the form of a bird to monitor and intimidate me.

It was indeed a distressing situation. In response, I started fervently praying that the monitoring bird would meet its end, and I asked God to bring blindness and confusion into the enemy's camp. I literally called upon God to defend me and my family, praying that the Lord would thwart the enemy's assignment.

A few days later, as I was leaving the house for an errand, I typically wouldn't use the front door for any reason. However, on that particular morning, the Holy Spirit prompted me to go through the front door. When I opened it, to my shock, I discovered a dead blackbird lying right on the steps leading to the front door.

Tears welled up, and I was trembling because I recognized that this was an act by the enemy, but the Lord had intervened and disrupted their plans. Unfortunately, the ordeal wasn't over at that point. However, I realized I was in a war that the Lord was teaching me to fight. Psalm 18:34 says, "He teaches my hands to make war, So that my arms can bend a bow of bronze."

TRAINING MY HANDS FOR WAR

"He teaches my hands to make war, So that my arms can bend a bow of bronze."

—Psalm 18:34

A few months later, as we were packing to officially put our house up for sale, I received a call from my insurance company. I had a general liability insurance policy, and they informed me about a potential lawsuit that was in the works. They were keen on gathering all the details from me. I shared what I knew, emphasizing that I wasn't physically present when the incident occurred.

Throughout this period, I received perhaps one or two letters from my insurance company regarding the issue, but nothing that raised major concerns. Eventually, we sold our house in November of that year, and we relocated to a different state.

Three weeks after relocating to a new state, my mailbox started overflowing with numerous letters from various lawyers claiming that I was being sued for a specific incident. The lady who had fallen at the vendor event had provided her statement and was now suing me for thousands of dollars, citing her injury from the fall.

To make matters more unsettling, strangers began showing up at our door when we were not home, attempting to serve me legal papers. The accusation that we had moved away from our previous state to evade the lawsuit was heartbreaking, but it was a baseless lie.

Throughout January, my mailbox continued to overflow with an avalanche of letters from attorneys. Eventually, the insurance company assigned me a lawyer to assist me in navigating this grueling process. This marked the beginning of a challenging two-year ordeal. I couldn't be my usual self; I felt I was constantly under surveillance.

After receiving the official lawsuit documents, I initially met with my lawyer to discuss the details of the lawsuit. To my surprise, I was instructed not to share any details about the case with anyone, including my husband. It was a rather perplexing directive, and I thought, "Hmm, I live with my husband. Who will I talk to if I can't confide in him about what I'm going through?" Additionally, I had to distance myself from social media to reduce my exposure to those platforms.

I turned even more fervently to the Holy Spirit for guidance during this period. Not that He hadn't been guiding me before, but this time it felt different. I realized there was no plan B; He was my one and ONLY hope. I needed to learn to listen to Him every moment and not miss His instructions. In response, I began praying and fasting despite the challenging circumstances.

The situation was especially daunting because we had recently relocated to a completely unfamiliar state with no acquaintances. We were essentially strangers in a new state, a new city, and a new church. Fear consumed me as I grappled with the entirety of this challenging situation.

Amidst this two-year ordeal, the Lord imparted the strategies I'm about to reveal. But before diving into those strategies, I'm sure you're curious about how this entire ordeal unfolded.

Not only was I facing a lawsuit from the lady who had fallen, but I also found myself targeted by the lawyers representing the venue where the event had taken place. I received a letter from their law firm, claiming that I owed them $18,000 and counting, citing the extensive time they had devoted to this case. Additionally, depending on when the case concluded, I would be responsible for covering all their attorney fees. It was an overwhelming situation, to say the least.

Throughout this entire ordeal, my solace was found in God. The house we were renting had a spare room that the owner had designated for prayer. I transformed that room into what I later referred to as a "war room." This room served as my prayer room, where I went to "war in prayer" on a daily basis, sometimes multiple times a day.

As I mentioned in the previous chapter, I felt like I could only cry out to God and, of course, confide in my husband; we were in this together. God became my unwavering anchor, and I leaned on Him like never before.

One Saturday morning, my husband took the kids to the grocery store, giving me some much-needed solitude. When they left the house, I collapsed onto the kitchen floor, screaming at the top of my lungs, asking why and what to do next. I cried for a whole hour, pleading with God to help me navigate this overwhelming situation.

By this point, my insurance company had contacted me and informed me that my insurance couldn't cover the lawsuit because I wasn't physically present when the incident happened. I had played no active role except for signing for the venue.

However, because I had signed up for the venue, I was being sued alongside the other young lady who took my spot at the vendor event. The young lady had no insurance, so her lawyers were attempting to shift the blame onto me. It was an absolute mess of a situation!

After that emotional outpouring, the Lord gently reminded me of the immense power in the words that come out of my mouth. He urged me to remember the importance of taking control of my thoughts, citing 2 Corinthians 10:5-6: "Casting down arguments and every high thing that exalts itself against the knowledge of God, bringing every thought into captivity to the obedience of Christ, and being ready to punish all disobedience when your obedience is fulfilled."

Furthermore, the Lord emphasized the profound potency of His Word. He encouraged me to focus on reciting His Word in my mind rather than dwelling on the words and threats of the adversary.

Lastly, He brought to mind Exodus 14:13-14: "And Moses said to the people, 'Do not be afraid. Stand still and see the salvation of the LORD, which He will accomplish for you today. For the Egyptians whom you see today, you shall see again no more forever. The LORD will fight for you, and you shall hold your peace.'"

These reminders were crucial for me and provided a wellspring of strength and hope during that challenging time.

I clung to these verses each time I received another piece of mail from a lawyer, and it wasn't just the lawyer representing the lady who had fallen at the event. There were also lawyers representing the essential oil company and the lawyers representing the venue. I found myself facing the challenges posed by four different law firms.

To help me navigate this tumultuous period, I turned to the Word of God in search of a story resembling my own situation. I began to meditate on that story and used it to guide how I approached my prayers.

I was so encouraged by the story of King Hezekiah. This story is shared in three different places: 2 Chronicles 32, 2 Kings 19, and Isaiah 37. It's the story of Hezekiah, when Sennacherib, king of Assyria, tried to intimidate and threaten him. Hezekiah prayed after he received the letter from the messengers. He went up to the house of the Lord and spread it out before HIM.

In 2 Kings 19:15-19, Hezekiah prayed before the LORD and said, "O LORD God of Israel, *the One* who dwells *between* the cherubim, You are God, You alone, of all the kingdoms of the earth. You have made heaven and earth. Incline Your ear, O Lord, and hear; open Your eyes, O LORD, and see; and hear the words of Sennacherib, which he has sent to reproach the living God. Truly, LORD, the kings of Assyria have laid waste the nations and their lands, and have cast their gods into the fire; for they *were* not gods, but the work of men's hands—wood and stone. Therefore they destroyed them. Now therefore, O LORD our God, I pray, save us from his hand, that all the kingdoms of the earth may know that You *are* the LORD God, You alone."

And God answered him through Prophet Isaiah: "I have heard your prayers concerning Sennacherib. Because of their rage and their arrogance, I will send you back the way you came." Verses 32-34, "'He shall not come into this city, Nor shoot an arrow there, Nor come before it with shield, Nor build a siege mound against it. By the way that he came, By the same shall he return; and he shall not come into this city,' says the LORD. 'For I will defend this city, to save it …'"

I immediately immersed myself in that story. I placed all the letters, all the threats, and the intimidation tactics—every single one of them—before the Lord. I prayed the same prayers that Hezekiah had prayed, believing with all my heart that the Lord would defend and fight for me, just as He had done for King Hezekiah. After all, the Bible reminds us that we are kings and priests unto the Lord (Revelations 1:6). If He had done it for King Hezekiah, I believed He would do it for me, too.

The Word of God filled me with tremendous hope. I understood that my Heavenly Father was training me to engage in a righteous battle that ONLY He could ultimately win. Yet, in His wisdom, He chose to invite me to be a part of the war strategy so that I could, in turn, teach others how to emerge victorious.

I received another letter from my lawyer shortly after that, indicating that a court date was being scheduled. I felt a bit disheartened. I didn't want to travel back to Pennsylvania for a court appearance, and the thought of testifying against the young lady who was at the event at the time of the incident weighed heavily on me.

My lawyer called me and began preparing me for the deposition, warning me that it would be a grueling experience. He cautioned me that the opposing lawyers would attempt to corner me into admitting fault and employ various intimidating tactics.

Throughout this trying time, I continued to pray and fast, constantly reminding the Lord of His promises. Then, something remarkable happened. I had a night vision. I was abruptly awakened around 4 a.m. I distinctly heard these words loud and clear: "Call those things that are not as though they were!" "Call those things that are not as though they were!" "Call those things that are not as though they were!" It repeated three times.

I sat up in bed and exclaimed, "Who was that? Who said that?" I glanced at my husband lying next to me, and he was fast asleep. I got up and walked to the bathroom, thinking, "That had to be the Lord." The voice was so loud it awakened me from sleep. This marked the first time I had ever heard an audible voice of the Lord. It was clear to me that God was imparting a strategy to face the next phase of this battle.

That morning, I received a profound revelation. Instead of merely asking the Lord to end these trials, I began asking Him to teach me how to wage this battle. I started requesting, "Reveal the strategies to me, Lord." It dawned on me that it's crucial to discern the season I was in and, equally important, to understand what actions are required. This insight reminded me of the sons of Issachar in 1 Chronicles 12:32, who had the understanding of the times and knew what Israel ought to do. Their wisdom guided them in their actions.

Psalm 18:31-34:
"For who is God, except the LORD?
And who is a rock, except our God?
It is God who arms me with strength,
And makes my way perfect.
He makes my feet like the feet of deer,
And sets me on my high places.
He teaches my hands to make war,
So that my arms can bend a bow of bronze."

SUPERNATURAL BLUEPRINT FOR WINNING IN ALL AREAS OF LIFE

And the Lord answered me with the following strategies.

Strategy 1: *The Word*

"'Is not My word like a fire?' says the Lord, 'And like a hammer that breaks the rock in pieces?'" (Jeremiah 23:29). If you delve into the original definition of the word "rock," you'll find that it means stronghold. The word of God holds immense power and is the key to shattering strongholds in your life.

Referring to Psalm 138:2, I recognized that the Lord had elevated His Word above everything, even above His own name. Understanding, believing, and firmly standing on His Word would be absolutely paramount during this season.

"In the beginning was the Word, and the Word was with God, and the Word was God" (John 1:1). This is because the Word is essentially God Himself. I understood that it wasn't enough to merely be acquainted with the Word; I needed to believe His Word. To win this battle, I had to believe in His Word so I could STAND on it! When I stand on the Word, I am, in essence, standing on God Himself, His faithfulness, His power, His authority, and His truth. Nothing can withstand the might of His Word. I needed to internalize this lesson; it was the first lesson He taught me.

"By faith, we understand that the worlds were framed by the Word of God, so that the things which are seen were not made of things which are visible."

If you investigate the word "framed" in your concordance, you'll discover its meanings include mending what has been broken, strengthening, putting things in order to completion, and making something that it ought to be. This insight reveals that I can mend, put in order, and shape my world using the Word of God.

And so, I began to put this understanding into practice by specifically praying God's Word. For example, during a crisis in marriage or finances, one might pray, "By faith, my marriage is strengthened, put back in order, and mended by the Word of God."

The Lord impressed upon me the need to be specific in my prayers. He instructed me not to offer general prayers. Just as Moses and Joshua were very specific in their prayers, I followed suit. I prayed with precision, asking for particular outcomes.

For instance, I expressed my desire not to have to go to court to testify or face a judge and jury. Due to the ongoing case, I didn't want to leave my family behind to stay in a hotel in another state for an indeterminate period. I was meticulous in my requests. I anchored my prayers in the truths found in the stories of Hezekiah from the Bible and the story of Balaam in

Numbers 23, which the Lord revealed to me during the lawyers' attempts to schedule the deposition.

Furthermore, the Lord directed me to turn my prayers into decrees. Instead of continually asking and begging, I learned to align with God's will and declare those things that are not as though they were.

In addition to the Word of God, He taught me about the power of my words. Jesus said, "For by your words you will be justified, and by your words you will be condemned" (Matt 12:37).

I realized that the words that come out of my mouth during this season are very important. Words make or break us. Life and death are in the power of our tongues, and we will eat the fruit of the words we speak. Personally, I believe the words we utter today can shape the reality of our future. This is what the Bible means when it says you will eat the fruit of your words.

Our family decided to conduct our unique version of Dr. Masaru's Rice Experiment. We wanted to demonstrate the impact of our words to our children during this season. Quite frankly, I was struggling to believe that my words matter. So the Lord prompted me to do this experiment.

We began by taking three jars and filling them with dry rice. Each jar received an equal amount of water. They were labeled as follows:

1. "Speak Life"
2. "Speak Death"
3. "Ignore"

Every day, I took the "Speak Life" jar to a different room and spoke "life words" over it, such as "I love you," "You are amazing," and "God has a plan for your life." Afterward, I returned it to the kitchen.

Next, I picked up the "Speak Death" jar and, in a separate room, uttered "negative words" like "I hate you," "You are an idiot," "You are stupid," You'll never make it," "You are going to lose this one."

The third jar, labeled "Ignore," was left untouched throughout this experiment.

We continued this routine for about three weeks, and the results were astonishing.

The "Speak Life" jar showed signs of fermentation but had no rot or mold.

In stark contrast, the "Speak Death" jar emitted a foul and disgusting odor, had mold growth, and was rotten.

Even the jar we completely ignored had an unpleasant smell and some mold.

This experiment made it very clear that words are immensely powerful.

I couldn't believe my words had caused mold to grow over the rice. And the one that I had spoken "life" over had no mold, nor did it have any odor. WOW!

Needless to say, this experiment put the fear of God in all of us. We were determined to choose our words wisely. Words can bless us or curse us. We are literally a product of the words we speak. So, the Lord taught me how to make words work for me by choosing to fill my words with purpose, power, and profit.

Words are like seeds; we must plant good ones. Speak what you desire to see come to fruition, not the opposite!

Strategy 2: *Prayer + Prophesy + Decree*

Sometimes, the Lord wants us to go through the battle instead of taking us out of it. It is there that He reveals to us: He is our ever-present help in times of trouble. Like in 2 Chronicles 20, Jehoshaphat and his armies still had to go through the battle and use the strategy the Lord gave them through a prophet. The Lord told them they would win the battle but still had to be involved in it.

Sometimes, God won't just take away the problems and allow them to vanish into the "never ever return island"… Nah … He's a good father. He wants His children to go through it while He walks with them. How would we ever know that He is a deliverer if we never have anything we need to be delivered from?

I really believe it's because He wants to train our hands to war while He shows Himself to be strong on our behalf. He is training an army, not a bunch of weaklings. The Israelites had to engage in several battles before they could take their promised land.

So, let's talk about prayer. The Lord told me you've got to learn how to ask for what you want. Moses did. A great example is when the Lord said He would destroy the Israelites for their murmuring and complaining. Moses reminded God of His character and was very specific about what he was asking God. Joshua 6 tells us that Joshua was very bold in His asking.

On the day that the Lord gave the Amorites over to the Israelites, Joshua spoke to the Lord in the presence of Israel: "'Sun, stand still over Gibeon; and Moon, in the Valley of Aijalon.' So the sun stood still, and the moon stopped, Till the people had revenge upon their enemies. Is this not written in the Book of Jasher? So the sun stood still in the midst of heaven, and did not hasten to go down for about a whole day" (Joshua 10:12-13).

If this verse were not written in the Bible, you and I would not have believed it could ever happen. In other words, God broke His own rules to fight for the people of Israel. The same way He would fight for you and me if you'd let Him have His way. He is a God who breaks protocols!

So, my strategy was to use the Word of God to pray. I was very intentional and specific about what I was asking God for. I was not shy about asking for what I wanted to see. I'd go from praying to declaring the Word of God over the lawsuit.

Some Christians get religious about what to ask God for. If it's in the Bible, then you are free to ask. Ask, and it shall be given to you. Don't be shy about asking your heavenly father. Sometimes, our upbringing prevents us from asking God because we are used to not being cared for by others or by our parents. And because people have told us "no" so many times, we don't know how to ask God for the things we desire. May I encourage you to not only ask, but ask BIG! You serve a BIG AND MIGHTY GOD.

James 5:17 says Elijah was a man just like us. But yet, He prayed earnestly that it would not rain, and it did not rain on the land for three and a half years. Again, he prayed, the heavens gave rain, and the earth yielded crops.

In other words, Prophet Elijah was just like us. He was subject to passions like us. He had feelings, too; he got angry at times, was scared at times, and was probably not very nice at times. I don't know, maybe? He was human! Yet, he prayed and prophesied that there wouldn't be rain for three and half years, and there was no rain. Then he prayed and prophesied that there would be rain, and it rained, and the earth brought forth her fruit! In the same way, we have to pray and prophesy our next season. So, I prophesied a season of favor and victory.

Prayer is an incredibly powerful tool. It is, in essence, a two-way conversation with the Lord. It's essential never to treat it as a one-way communication; instead, expect the Lord to speak to you during your prayers. Have your Bible with you during prayer whenever possible, for the Holy Spirit wants to communicate with you through His Word. When you are praying, here are three types of prayer to include in your time with the Lord: Prayer of Repentance, Prayer of Worship, and War Prayers (pray in tongues as well as in your native language).

Prophecies represent God's will and intentions for us. The most profound prophecy you can access is the Word of God itself. It's important to refrain from reaching out to so-called "prophets" via direct messages, asking them to prophesy over you, or even worse, inquiring if they have a word for you. This practice is not aligned with God's ways. Instead, you should learn how to hear from God for yourself. As the Bible states, "My sheep hear My voice, and I know them, and they follow Me" (John 10:27).

I prayed fervently in my prayer language. I mean, with great intensity! If you haven't received the gift of speaking in tongues, I encourage you to seek the Holy Spirit for this gift. It's crucial because there are times when we don't know what to pray, and in those moments, the Spirit intercedes on our behalf. Eventually, we may run out of words in our native language. Praying in tongues allows us to pray for God's mysteries and perfect will. Personally, I want to align my prayers with God's will at all times. So, while you should pray in your native language, switch to your heavenly language when your words run dry, according to Romans 8:26-28.

Decrees involve audibly speaking statements of truth as we align ourselves with God's will and His purposes for our lives. I love this definition from Jennifer Eivaz, "Decree is making a statement of truth that carries the authority of a court order." Decreeing is a powerful tool in bridging the gap between what God intends for us and our current reality. By making decrees, we place a demand on God, holding onto His promises outlined in His Word. It's a proactive stance with two parts. As we make decrees, we not only establish God's purposes in our lives but also actively confront and dismantle any opposition that dares to stand against what we are working to establish.

We dabar (speak) His will concerning a situation according to His Word. Why? Because the kingdom of God is voice-activated. When you begin to speak the life-giving Word of God, you will see it bloom all around you. The Holy Spirit showed me that combining these three powerful elements is akin to deploying a bomb squad into the enemy's camp.

He instructed me to start agreeing with His Word, so I began to decree the Word of the Lord as if it had already come to pass. Do you know why the Lord encourages us to do this? It's because it boosts our faith. It propels us into action, shifting us from a victim mentality to praying from a position of victory.

You may have noticed in the Bible that when Jesus prayed, His prayers were often concise and filled with authority. For instance, He would say things like "Be healed," "Rise up and pick up your mat," or "Go, you have been made whole."

His prayers were not lengthy and drawn out. While there's nothing wrong with lengthy prayers, especially in public settings, when Jesus prayed in such situations, He made short decrees as if the outcome had already been accomplished. We may not know the exact nature of His private prayers when He would withdraw early in the morning to commune with His Father. However, Jesus had unwavering confidence that the Father heard Him.

The Lord instructed me to pray similarly. He encouraged me to thank the Father beforehand, just as Jesus did. So, I prayed, "Father, I thank you that I will not have to go to court to testify against the young lady. I thank you that, just as you spoke to the donkey in Numbers 22, you will speak to the lawyers in the middle of the night. I thank you that my insurance company will change their stance and agree to cover me. I thank you that I will not have to pay a dime to the lawyers or anyone else."

With tears in my eyes and on my face, I poured out my heart before the Lord, offering thanks for everything and anything related to this case. Every fear and tormenting word that the enemy had whispered into my ears, I transformed into prayers of thanksgiving. Honestly, this was the only way I could function during that season.

The Bible in Job 22:28 (KJV) tells us, "Thou shalt also decree a thing, and it shall be established unto thee: and the light shall shine upon thy ways." The word "light" in Hebrew signifies the light of instruction and the light of prosperity. In essence, when you decree the Word of God, it becomes established, and you receive divine instruction. Your answer lies within the pages of His Word. Ask God to open your eyes to see the well of His wisdom surrounding you.

Strategy 3: *Fasting*

Fasting was another strategy the Lord revealed to me. I am well aware of the power of fasting. Fasting humbles you; it's a means of crucifying the desires of the flesh. It accelerates change, strips away pride, and brings hidden issues to the surface. Additionally, fasting rejuvenates you. Recognizing that I was in a spiritual battle, I chose to push aside my plate and engage in fasting multiple times during this challenging period.

Fasting, as described in Isaiah 58, offers clarity. A biblical fast involves abstaining from food, not the type of fast that pertains to social media or other non-food-related activities. While consecration, which includes fasting from things like TV or social media, has its place, I'm referring to a fast where you abstain from food for a set number of days. Always be led by the Holy Spirit in this regard. I willingly submitted myself to fasting during this season.

Let's examine Isaiah 58:6-11, which is my favorite passage in the Bible when it comes to understanding what to do and avoid during a fast:

"Is this not the fast that I have chosen: To loose the bonds of wickedness, To undo the heavy burdens, To let the oppressed go free, And that you break every yoke? ... Then your light shall break forth like the morning, Your healing shall spring forth speedily, And your righteousness shall go before you; The glory of the LORD shall be your rear guard. Then you shall call, and the LORD will answer; You shall cry, and He will say, 'Here I am.' If you take away the yoke from your midst, The pointing of the finger, and speaking wickedness, If you extend your soul to the hungry And satisfy the afflicted soul, Then your light shall dawn in the darkness, And your darkness shall be as the noonday. The LORD will guide you continually, And satisfy your soul in drought, And strengthen your bones; You shall be like a watered garden, And like a spring of water, whose waters do not fail."

These verses reveal the Lord's promise to provide guidance and clear instructions. The word "light" in the phrase "your light shall dawn in the darkness" signifies "light of instructions" in Hebrew. This means the Lord will guide us and provide instructions even in times of darkness. I needed the Lord's guidance and clear instructions on how to pray and what actions to take.

Let me ask you a question: Do you need specific and clear guidance in your life right now? May I suggest pushing aside your plate for a period of time to help you get clarity? If anything, it will humble you. As the Lord promised, He will not despise a broken and contrite spirit.

Following a period of fasting, the Lord directed me to specific scriptures to pray daily. Fasting acts as a catalyst, expediting spiritual growth and bringing about transformative change.

Strategy 4: *Communion*

Taking Communion was the next strategy the Lord revealed I needed. The Bible tells us, "And when He had given thanks, He broke it and said, Take, eat; this is my body which is broken for you: do this in remembrance of Me" (1 Cor. 11:24).

Jesus didn't specify that we should only take communion once a month at church. The Lord taught me the significance of taking communion regularly, although it's essential to always be led by the Holy Spirit in this practice.

The blood that Jesus shed on the cross serves multiple purposes. It not only cleanses us from all unrighteousness (1 John 1:7), but it also justifies us as if we had never sinned. Because of the blood of Jesus Christ, we are justified, acquitted, made righteous, declared not guilty, and made right as if we had never sinned.

In Hebrews 12:22-24, it's explained that the blood of Jesus speaks a better word than that of Abel. Abel's blood cried out for vengeance because he was killed by his brother, Cain. However, the blood of the Son of the living God speaks mercy, mercy, mercy! For about a year, I took communion nearly every day and made these confessions:

- Jesus, you were broken so that I can be whole.
- You were emptied so that I can be full.
- You were despised so that I can be accepted.
- You were rejected so that I can be celebrated.
- You bore affliction so that I can be healed.
- You became poor so that I can be rich.

Jesus did everything in the opposite way so that I could step into the blessings available to me. Taking communion, for me, was like opening the gates of heaven. I rejoiced daily because it reminded me that Jesus had granted me access to the throne room of God through His sacrifices for me. During this season of taking communion daily, I was delivered from the spirit of rejection and the orphan spirit. The truth set me free.

This was the season when I stepped into the role of a daughter in His kingdom. The Greek word for daughter means "acceptable to God" and "rejoicing in His peculiar care." The Lord taught me that I could come to Him with anything and everything. He said, "Daughter, I want you to be yourself. You don't have to pretend to be anyone else. I love your passion and your boldness. I made you just like that."

This moment of realization set me free. Before this, I was in deep bondage and self-hatred. I had prayed to God many times to let me die because I didn't want to live anymore due to the pain and trauma I had experienced at a young age. It took this challenging trial for me to understand that God Himself loved me. All the rejections, anger, hatred, misery, and doubts began to fall away from my soul. I desperately needed this transformation to redeem my perspective of the trial.

Strategy 5: *Praise and Worship*

This is a powerful secret passcode to enter the throne room of God: Psalm 100:4 says, "Enter into His Gates with thanksgiving, And into His Courts with praise ..." This key unlocks prison doors, as illustrated in Acts 16 when Paul and Silas were locked in a jail cell. They worshipped God at midnight, and suddenly, their chains broke, and the doors opened. Praise and worship hold great power; they are your secret weapons against the enemy.

In 2 Chronicles chapter 20, we see another example when the Moabites and Ammonites were coming against Jehoshaphat and his armies. Their battle plan was to worship, and as they did, God sent a sudden attack on their enemies, causing them to turn and destroy one another. Worship can release a sudden attack on your enemies. So, I would worship God with praise, and sometimes, as a prophetic act, I would dance around my room while singing at the top of my lungs. I raised a Hallelujah in the presence of my enemies. It was like shooting arrows into the enemy's camp.

The Hebrew definition of "Hallelujah" is to praise, boast, and act like a madman. Isn't it interesting? The Lord is encouraging you to praise Him wholeheartedly without being concerned about the opinions of others. Don't let anyone restrict your worship of God. Worship Him freely because He is worthy of it all. Your worship is a weapon of war in your mouth.

Thank Him, the One who sits in the circle of the earth. Thank Him, the One who asked, "Is there anything too difficult for Him?" Thank Him, the One who promised, "I will give you beauty for ashes, the oil of joy for mourning, the garment of praise for the spirit of heaviness. For your shame, you shall have double." Praise Him even when you haven't yet seen the physical manifestation of what you've been asking for. Praise Him in anticipation of your desired outcome. I can't help but add one more key strategy to unlock the door to unusual breakthroughs in your life.

Strategy 6: *Faith*

Faith is the substance of things hoped for. What you hope for and your expectation matters to God because as a man thinks, so is he. You literally become your thoughts.

Recall the story when Moses sent 12 men to scout the land God promised them. They returned with a good report, but 10 out of the 12 men had different expectations of what would happen if they attempted to take the land promised by the Lord. They lacked hope because fear had gripped their hearts. They focused on the GIANTS and the size of the fortified cities.

In contrast, Joshua and Caleb had different hearts and higher expectations. They believed that since God had shown His power when He parted the Red Sea and defeated their enemies, He would come through for them again. Their hope was in God's ability to deliver, not in the GIANTS. To experience an unusual breakthrough, we must raise our expectations.

Hebrews 12:1-2 says, "Therefore we also, since we are surrounded by so great a cloud of witnesses, let us lay aside every weight, and the sin which so easily ensnares us, and let us run with endurance the race that is set before us, looking unto Jesus, the author and finisher of our faith, who for the joy that was set before Him endured the cross, despising the shame, and has sat down at the right hand of the throne of God."

Jesus endured the cross because He anticipated the joy of us seated with Him in heavenly places. He looked forward to you boldly entering His throne room to seek help and mercy. He endured the shame of the cross because He anticipated you being with Him forever, knowing that nothing could separate you from His love. He endured the pain of the cross because He saw you before you were even formed and wanted to spend eternity with you. He said yes to your destiny!

In response to this, we should lay aside doubt, the "sin" that easily entangles us, by focusing on the desired outcome. This is how you gain the power to endure. Pay attention to your thought patterns, for you will eventually become what you think. You must raise your expectations as a child of the Most High God. Believe that He is a good Father who wants to bless you despite the challenges and giants you may face.

YOU CAN HAVE WHATSOEVER YOU SAY

"For assuredly, I say to you, whoever says to this mountain, 'Be removed and be cast into the sea,' and does not doubt in his heart, but believes that those things he says will be done, he will have whatever he says."

—Mark 11:23

A full year passed, and the Lord had imparted numerous lessons to me. I realized that I could no longer align myself with fear. During this period, I immersed myself in my Bible, reading it cover to cover. I was determined not to be defeated by this situation. Throughout this time, I experienced a multitude of dreams. I'll share one of them with you because it is significant to this story. Oh, by the way, we had relocated to a new house amidst this entire ordeal. Now, let's delve into the dream:

In the dream, I found myself in my kitchen, and a Caucasian lady was assisting me in opening my mail. She picked up a black envelope adorned with gold lettering, and her expression immediately turned to one of concern. I observed her face and asked why she appeared so worried as she handed me the envelope. She didn't reply, so I took the envelope from her and noticed it had my lawyer's address.

Upon opening it, I discovered a letter stating that I had been granted one hundred and twenty-something thousand dollars to purchase something or use it as I wished. I looked at the lady and said, "This is fantastic news. Why were you so concerned?"

Then, I woke up. To be honest, I didn't quite grasp the meaning of the dream at that time. I prayed over it for a while but eventually set it aside due to the overwhelming events occurring. The lawyers were in frequent meetings, and my communication with my lawyer had escalated to a few times a week. The deposition date had been finalized, and I couldn't avoid it any longer. My lawyer and I had numerous phone calls to prepare me for the dreaded day.

I remember uttering a prayer, saying, "Father, please spare me from this 'cup.' I don't want to face seven lawyers only to be grilled, torn apart, and cornered!"

He explained to me that they aimed to make me a "scapegoat" and that they wanted me to bear the cost of the injury, medical expenses, and all the lawyers' fees. They wished to find me guilty!

My response was simply, "Okay, Lord! I know you have a plan to deliver me from this!"

So, it was crucial to thoroughly prepare myself to ensure I didn't say the wrong thing at the wrong time. After numerous phone calls during which my lawyer coached me on what to say and avoid, the day of the deposition finally arrived. I had to drive to the city alone because, as you know, I was in a new state and didn't know anyone I could trust to watch my kids. Consequently, my husband had to stay home with them while they were homeschooled.

For a few moments here, I allowed my flesh to take over and began to think about all the things that could go wrong during this deposition. I became TERRIFIED! The night before, I cried my eyes out, screamed, and vented my frustration at the devil. But then, I calmed down when I realized this "cup" wasn't going anywhere. I felt like the Lord was silent that night.

Suddenly, His Word came to me and reminded me of Psalm 24:8-10. I consciously chose to place my TRUST in Jehovah Gibbor—The Lord Strong and Mighty, the One who is mighty in battle and has never lost a single one. **Let me clarify some important cultural differences:** In Jewish culture, traditionally, fathers raised up their sons to take over the family business. In contrast, in Western culture, parents often say, "I support your choice, no matter what, even if it's a bit unconventional. You want to be a poop sweeper, I'll support you."

While supporting your children's dreams is perfectly fine, I'd like to emphasize the Jewish approach for the sake of this comparison. Jewish parents don't typically ask their children what they want to become when they grow up. Instead, they raise them to inherit and manage the family business, nurturing them to be warriors.

This upbringing is reflected in Psalm 127:4-5, which describes children as "arrows in the hand of a warrior, So are the children of one's youth. Happy is the man who fills his quiver full of them; They shall not be ashamed, But shall speak with their enemies in the gate."

Essentially, the expectation is for the sons to face their fathers' enemies rather than the other way around. This contrasts with the Western world, where fathers often handle conflicts on behalf of their children.

However, God was trying to teach me a different perspective. Instead of asking Him to fight this particular battle, He reminded me of the story of Moses at the Red Sea. When Moses cried out to God as the Egyptians approached them at the Red Sea, the Lord replied, "Why are you standing there calling out to me? Go forward, raise your staff, stretch out your hand, and divide the sea" (Exodus 14:15-16).

The Lord was conveying that I have been prepared for a purpose. I have been raised for such a time as this. I have been anointed for this battle. My hands have been trained for war. So, rather than waiting and hoping God will show up and put a stop to the whole mess, I should take action and face the war head-on.

I woke up early that morning to spend some time with the Lord, hoping to hear Him tell me that this was a bad dream and would soon be over. However, reality hit hard. As I got ready to leave, I heard Him whisper, "You are not alone. I'm going with you." These words, reassuring as they were, provided the peace I needed.

Upon arriving at the location, I spoke to my lawyer on the phone. He told me what color suit he would be wearing so that I could recognize him on the video screen. The process began with the swearing-in, and then the grueling questions commenced. For four hours, I did my best to answer all the questions. To my surprise, I managed to hold up quite well until the very last few minutes when one of the lawyers began twisting my words to change their meaning. It became frustrating, so I remained silent and replied, "I'm sorry, I don't know the answer to that." That became my response to the rest of his questions. When he realized I wasn't providing much more to work with, all seven lawyers unanimously decided to end the session.

Afterward, I felt so numb that I couldn't speak for hours. I couldn't even tell my husband how it all went. I went straight to bed and slept for a solid 12 hours. The next day, my lawyer called me and told me to expect a substantial transcript folder. He instructed me to go through it line by line, make any necessary corrections, and return it to him within a couple of days because these documents would be crucial when we go to court.

Let me be honest; this is when I reached my breaking point. As soon as I hung up the phone, I practically tossed it aside and went to the basement to have a heart-to-heart with God. And the Holy Spirit said in Mark 11:23: "For assuredly, I say to you, whoever says to this mountain, 'Be removed and be cast into the sea,' and does not doubt in his heart, but believes that those things he says will be done, he will have whatever he says." In my mind, I took this as if the Lord was saying to me,

"Lara, you can have whatsoever you say!" You better believe I did exactly that!

I said, "Father, I am not going to court! I will not go through any more documents. This case has stolen so much from me. I haven't been able to confide in anyone about all the turmoil I've been enduring. I have been completely alone in this mess. I will not answer any more phone calls. I am done! Devil, listen carefully: this case is over now! I am done with these manipulations from the devil and his minions."

I cried, sobbed, yelled, and then cried some more because, you know ... And then, I picked myself up. I wiped my tears and said, "Jesus, it's over! I declare this to be over!" I went upstairs and got something to eat. During this season, I lost so much weight because I completely lost my appetite.

Then came the 2020 lockdown. The world was brought to a standstill for several months. During this time, I hadn't received any updates from my lawyer since the last phone call the day after the deposition. Honestly, I didn't even feel the need to call him. The ONLY thing I did during this time was to continue to confess out of my mouth exactly what I wanted because the Lord said, "Lara, you can have whatsoever you say," according to Mark 11:23. I took this word seriously as if my life depended on it. Quite frankly, it did!

Then, on a Tuesday afternoon, September 17th, my phone rang while I was sitting in the car, waiting for my kids to come out of their dental appointment. I glanced at the phone, and it was my lawyer. I gasped for air ... It had been nine months since I heard from him. I picked up the phone and said:

Me: Hello, Mr. Lawyer.

Lawyer: Hey Lara, how are you doing? How have you been?

Me: I'm doing well. And you?

Lawyer: Great! I have some good news and some bad news. Which one do you want first?

Me: Ahem ... the good news.

Lawyer: Well, the attorney for the prosecutor (the lady that fell) called me and gave me the following news. He spoke to the woman, and she has decided to withdraw the entire case, except that she would need you to cover all her medical expenses. Then, out of nowhere, your insurance company called and said they will cover all her medical expenses in the total amount of approximately $120K. The case has now been canceled, and you are not responsible for anything. It is over!

Me: Whaaaaaaaaaaaat?! I gasped!

Lawyer: Yes, it's all over! The bad news is you should expect a letter in the mail. I need you to sign it and return it to me ASAP. Sorry you have to get one more piece of mail from me. But after that, you are now free to live your life. It was nice meeting you.

I'm sorry it was under these circumstances. Do you have any questions for me?

Me: I am speechless. No, I don't have any questions. Thank you so much for all your help (as I held back tears).

Lawyer: You are welcome. Take care!

Me: SPEECHLESS!

"Oh my goodness, what just happened," I exclaimed as I ran across the parking lot like a madwoman. "Jesus, You are Faithful! Thank you, Father! Thank you for helping me. Thank you for fighting for me. Thank you for defending me. Oh my word, how do I begin to thank you!"

I was rendered speechless for hours! All I could do was cry and keep repeating, "Thank you, Jesus! The Judge of all Judges has ruled in my favor!"

Let's talk about the power of prayer and decrees! I would like to emphasize the miracles.

THE MIRACLES

"Call to Me, and I will answer you, and show you great and mighty things, which you do not know."

—*Jeremiah 33:3*

#1. The Insurance Company Assigned Me a Lawyer

As I mentioned, my insurance company assigned me a lawyer who lived in a different state. Our move out of state had occurred right at the beginning of the lawsuit. Despite never meeting me in person, this lawyer became my staunch advocate. I believe the Lord Himself appointed him to assist me in this ordeal. He fought tirelessly on my behalf, ensuring that I wouldn't have to leave my family to travel to Pennsylvania for days. He successfully postponed court dates and arranged for me to do the deposition via video, sparing me the burden of traveling to PA.

The other lawyers representing the venue sent me a bill stating that I was responsible for all their fees, as per the contract I signed to secure the venue. Miraculously, God took care of this matter as well, and I didn't have to pay a single dime.

#2. COVID-19 and Its Surprising Blessing

In 2020, the world was shaken by the COVID-19 pandemic, and it was undoubtedly a challenging time for everyone. However, strangely enough, it was a blessing in disguise for me. The pandemic caused significant delays in many aspects of life, and during this pause, God was able to work on the hearts of all the parties involved in my case.

Throughout this ordeal, I had taken some time to research the other lawyers involved in the case. I discovered that one of the attorneys representing the lady who was suing me had a Christian background or, at the very least, had grown up in a Christian home. I felt led to pray and ask the Lord to appear to him in a dream, just as He had done in the Bible, and speak to him about reconsidering his involvement in the case. I believed that if the Lord could communicate with a donkey, as we read in Numbers 26, He could surely reach this lawyer.

According to my lawyer, a remarkable turn of events occurred. The lady's lawyer had a conversation with her about certain matters, and as a result, she decided to withdraw the case. Evidently, the Holy Spirit had intervened and disrupted the enemy's plans.

#3. A Prophetic Dream Fulfilled

Recall the dream I shared about the Caucasian woman handing me my mail in my kitchen, which contained a letter stating that I was being given approximately $120,000 to use as I pleased. In Judges 7:13, the Lord granted a dream to the enemies, and Gideon was able to discern its interpretation.

This revelation gave him the courage to pursue the Midi-
anites because the Lord showed that Gideon would defeat
them. You can read this powerful account in the 7th chapter
of Judges.

Now, let's return to my dream. The dream that God gave me
became a reality. My insurance company, which had previ-
ously declined to cover me, miraculously stepped in. It just so
happened that the lady's medical expenses amounted to the
exact sum that the Lord had revealed to me in my dream.
WON'T GOD DO IT! There is absolutely nothing impossible
for our God! He is the King of Glory, the Lord Strong and
Mighty, the One who has never lost a battle!

I can boldly declare that the Word of God was alive and active
in every aspect of this testimony. I assure you, this is no exag-
geration! It's crazy until it happens!

#4. Get Ready for a Surprise!

Remember the unusual visitor at the beginning, the man in
the long black coat who came to my house in March 2018
for questioning? He left behind a business card with the lawyer's information that differed from the lawyers later involved
in the lawsuit against me. Why is this important, you ask? Well,
buckle up because here's where it gets interesting.

On June 1, 2018, during my quiet time with the Lord, I read 2
Chronicles 20. The entire chapter was like fire. Unbeknownst
to me, that morning, I highlighted verses 15-17. Little did I
know I would need them. Later that same day, the ominous

bird showed up at my house, and it was also the day of my daughter's dance recital, an event that nearly turned deadly.

After we got rid of the menacing bird, the man in the long black coat appeared at my doorstep as we left for the recital. However, the Lord told me not to answer the door and gave me specific instructions found in verses 16-17 of 2 Chronicles. It was a directive to position myself, stand still, and witness God's deliverance. These verses came to mind as I contemplated what to do with the man at my door, and I followed God's guidance. You likely know the rest of the story from that day.

But here's the kicker: the man in the long black coat and his company ended up not representing the lady who sued me. I don't know if she parted ways with them or, as I'd like to believe, the Lord removed them from the equation and brought in a different law firm. I thought it was interesting to note that I received the victory phone call on the 17th, and this entire time, the Lord had graciously given me an answer from verse 17 of 2 Chronicles 20.

#5. You Can Have Whatsoever You Say

This was a very important one for me. It has completely changed how I view the Word of God. The Lord, in his goodness, ensured that I got to this point where I understood the power of believing in his Word and the results of what happens when I agree with it and confess it. I was at the point where nothing was going to stop me from believing this verse.

The Lord opened my eyes to see something profound in the last part of Mark 11:23. Up until that time, I had never seen it. It says, "… he shall have whatsoever he says." I looked at that word in the NKJV and said out loud, "I can have whatsoever I say, Lord." It went so deep in my heart that nobody could convince me otherwise. I knew I had found something so significant it would change my life if I agreed with it. So I did; I said the words that I desired to see come to pass. I circled it so many times and confessed it.

In February 2020, I was reading my word, and the Lord reminded me again of the same verse, and I wrote in my Bible exactly the way I wanted to see this come to fruition. Seven months later, the Lord delivered me. I realized God gave me exactly what I had written in my Bible. It was all over!

I promised the Lord: "If you assist me and rescue me from this ordeal, I will share with the world what you have done for me."

Here I am ... sharing with you how He rescued me.

The answer was evident: "Position yourself, stand firm, and witness God's deliverance." The Lord was faithful in teaching me how to become the person He has designed me to be so that I can do the things I was created for.

I'm confident that the Lord, in His mercy, allowed me to go through this ordeal to reveal the gifts He placed inside me. He wanted me to recognize my capabilities and understand what I was made of. Childhood trauma had left me broken and doubting my worth and talents. Rejection had led me to hide my gifts. Through a transformative journey, the Lord guided me to rediscover and embrace my gifts.

In the next section of this book, I'll guide you on how to reprogram your mind, take your position, and discover your God-given talents. You'll learn how to use them not only within the church but also in your home and in the marketplace.

THE ANATOMY
OF TRANSFORMATION

*"And do not be conformed to this world, but be transformed
by the renewing of your mind, that you may prove what is
that good and acceptable and perfect will of God."*

—Romans 12:2

To transition from a setback to a comeback, a transformative process is essential. This involves letting go of pride and ego, humbling yourself before the Almighty God, and surrendering to His will.

While many Christian influencers on social media may showcase "Christianese" and wear God-related apparel, not all are genuinely spirit-filled. Some Christians knowingly or unknowingly engage in New Age practices, highlighting the importance of knowledge. As the Bible warns, "My people perish because of lack of knowledge," but it also emphasizes that "through knowledge shall the righteous be delivered." To navigate the process of transformation, it's crucial to be properly equipped with the right tools. We refer to this process as A.M.E. (Adopt, Mature, Empower).

Adopt

Consider this the foundational step of being fully accepted by God, the Father. It begins with repentance, turning away from sins, and embracing forgiveness. Confessing with your mouth and believing in your heart that Jesus Christ is Lord leads to a profound transformation.

In this stage, you are adopted into the family of Christ, becoming a new creation with old things passing away. As heirs with Christ, you belong to Him securely, and nothing can pluck you out of His loving hands. Even if you're already saved, Jesus calls you to be His hands and feet, sharing the hope found in Christ with others. It's essential to recognize that you can't earn God's love through impressive actions like reading the Bible multiple times a day or frequent prayers. God's love is freely given, and He is more interested in your motives, character, and how you reflect Christ each day.

Mature

The goal is to grow and mature into Christlikeness, transitioning from spiritual infancy to maturity. Moving from consuming to producing, equipping, and empowering others is vital. As you become a mature Christian, you shift from being taught to becoming a teacher, playing a role in the growth of others. This transformation is necessary for fulfilling your God-given purpose, whether in the marketplace, at home, or in the church. This phase involves personal development, as mentioned in Romans 12:2, emphasizing the renewal of the mind to manifest God's perfect will.

This transformation is crucial for understanding and recognizing what is good, pleasing, and the perfect will of God. It serves as a metamorphosis, essential for reprogramming your mind. The term "mind" encompasses various definitions, including being the seat of thoughts and memory. Oxford's dictionary defines it as the "inclination, tendency, or way of thinking and feeling; a specified kind of character, disposition, spirit, or temper." Strong's Dictionary defines the mind as a "particular way of thinking and judging thoughts, feelings, purposes, and desires, also the intellectual faculty, the understanding."

While God created us for success, many of us have been inadvertently programmed for failure by societal influences, individuals, and various factors. Parents, friends, media, school, church, pastors, past hurts, and more contribute to this programming. Your environment and the people you associate with significantly impact your mental programming. This programming often hinders your ability to succeed or fulfill your purpose.

Recognizing this challenge, the Bible instructs you to be transformed by the renewing of your mind. Without this transformation, your mind remains unstable, making it difficult to step into your God-given assignments. The transformation process follows the R3 Model (Recognize, Remove, and Replace), providing a structured approach to reprogramming the mind for success and purpose.

Recognize—First, you must be aware of what you may have been programmed with. A simple way to recognize this is if it doesn't line up with the truth of the word of God, then it must be discarded.

Remove the pattern—Now that you are aware of your negative programming, you must get rid of it. This is where it gets challenging for some. Jesus died to give you access to the power of the Holy Spirit. If you are going to do greater things than Jesus did while on earth, if you desire to be unleashed from a place of despair and hopelessness into a place of victory, then you need a superior power—the power of the Holy Spirit. This requires being intentional about where you want to go. If your current mindset is not serving you, you must do all you can to get rid of it.

Replace—The next crucial step in the transformation process is to replace limiting beliefs with the truth found within the scriptures and then take massive action toward your desires. Unfortunately, many within the church struggle with issues like limiting beliefs, a lack mindset, identity crises, and rejection.

The Lord is waiting for you to be set free so you can be released into your assignment with absolute clarity. If you need deliverance or inner healing, it's essential to actively pursue it so that you can be free to step into your calling.

In my journey, I dismantled the belief that I would never amount to anything or that life would always be a struggle. It began with a commitment to read the Bible cover to cover, not for a set time but with a purpose—to know God intimately and seek transformation. I wanted to know God for myself and not from what church folks told me about Him.

He says, "Those who know my name will put their trust in me." If I'm going to put my trust in Him, then the prerequisite is to know Him. There's no better way to know God than to read about His character in the Bible. It didn't matter how long it would take; I was determined to know Him because I was desperate for a transformation in my life. I needed to hear God speak to me directly through His Word.

Through this process, I discovered that the Bible is the ultimate success book, offering strategies for success in every aspect of life. It also revealed the stories of imperfect individuals God used powerfully in the marketplace, showcasing that miracles extend beyond the synagogue. I rediscovered my identity as a daughter of the Most High God. I also discovered that He gave each and every one of us gifts, and we are to use those gifts to serve one another. I realized that these gifts aren't confined to the church walls but are meant to be employed at home, as a wife and mom, and in the marketplace as an entrepreneur. Yeah, talk about a major transformation!

This transformation is only possible when you shift from a passive consumer to an active participant. It's time to take control of your life. Quit waiting on God because the truth of the matter is He is actually waiting on you to take action. He is waiting on you to start to believe His word. He is waiting on you, warrior. He is waiting on you to take your shield of faith to quench every fiery dart of the enemy of your soul. He is waiting on you to draw your sword of the Spirit, which is His word.

The world tells you, "You will always be depressed, busted, and oppressed." His Word says, "You will be transformed by the renewing of your mind." The world says, "You will always struggle in your finances." His Word says, "He gives you the ability to create wealth." Take the s(word) of God, cut through the lies of the enemy, and see that God himself has already gone ahead of you and won the victory for you. He has already sent Jesus to pave the way for you. The decision to take the necessary steps and become an action-taker will ultimately lead you to align with God's calling and purposes for your life. You were made to shine His light in this dark world, using your God-given gifts, talents, and skills to serve in the marketplace, at home, or wherever He has called you.

Empower

To step into your calling with confidence and assurance, you need to be empowered by the supernatural power of the Holy Spirit. I'll share a story about my mother's return to Nigeria after a seven-year absence, a journey that marked the beginning of our move to the US. It is a powerful testament to the impact of the supernatural power of the Holy Spirit. It vividly illustrates how being empowered and inspired by the Holy Spirit, particularly through prayer, led to a significant outcome—granting a visa to the US.

On a beautifully sunny day, a day etched permanently in my memory, we journeyed to the US embassy in Nigeria. Seven arduous years had passed, during which we lived with our father without our mother.

At the age of 10, I witnessed my mother being cast out of our home, practically naked, left to fend for herself. With the intention of returning for us, she embarked on a journey to the US to seek employment and support. However, what was initially planned as a one-year absence stretched into seven. She toiled diligently as a nurse, sponsored by the company she worked for, paralleling the biblical narrative of Jacob laboring for 14 years to wed Rachel.

My mother, in a similar vein, devoted seven years to securing sponsorship for herself and her six children. This meant leaving us in the care of our father while she pursued a better future. After completing these seven years, she returned with the assurance that we would be granted visas to leave the country.

Ecstatic at the prospect of escaping the hardships and poverty of the preceding years, we reached the embassy. There, we painstakingly submitted numerous documents, photos, and letters to establish our familial connection and dispel any notion of kidnapping.

However, our joy was short-lived. Despite our efforts, the embassy official expressed dissatisfaction with our documentation and, regrettably, decided not to grant us visas. Our collective hopes and dreams of leaving Nigeria for America were abruptly shattered.

With tears streaming down our faces, my mom, faced with the devastating news, gathered her six children and led us into one of the bathroom stalls, urging us to pray. In that cramped space, she turned to me, a 17-year-old who had immersed herself in memorizing Bible verses. When she asked me to lead, the Holy Spirit immediately brought to mind a verse from Proverbs 21:1: "The king's heart is in the hand of the Lord, like the rivers of water; He turns it wherever He wishes."

Drawing from that verse, I prayed for divine intervention, asking the Lord to turn the heart of the embassy official like rivers of water. The prayer, though brief, was sincere.

Returning to the waiting area, the official called us back to the window, this time to return our documents. As she stamped each passport with the approval of a visa granting entry to the US, elation flooded us. It was a miraculous moment, a prayer inspired by the Holy Spirit swiftly answered by the Lord. This marked the start of a strong connection with the Holy Spirit, empowering me with guidance, revelation, and more. The Holy Spirit is faithful, always guiding and revealing the truth when needed.

To have dominion, you must be empowered by the Holy Spirit, fueled by the fire of God. Succeeding in this world requires special, powerful **super**natural help, considering your struggles are not against flesh and blood but against principalities in high places.

In everyday life, like at home, in business, or in dealing with problems, it's crucial to have the Holy Spirit's guidance for wisdom. When tackling injustices, relying on the power of the Holy Spirit is key, and using the gifts of the Spirit is vital.

Your spiritual gifts are like superpowers in the marketplace. Clearly, defining the calling of God in your life is crucial. It allows you to align with your God-given assignment, bringing clarity. This alignment empowers you to step out of challenges and into a place of victory in all aspects of life—be it the marketplace, raising your kids at home, or engaging in ministry. God desires to equip you with His supernatural power to operate at a level that glorifies Him and establishes His purpose on earth.

*"... To Him who loved us and washed us from our sins in
His own blood, and has made us kings and priests to
His God and Father, to Him be glory and dominion forever
and ever. Amen."*

—Revelation 1:5-6

As kings and leaders that have been entrusted with spiritual gifts, our call extends beyond the walls of the church. Using your spiritual gifts demonstrates God's power not only at home and in the church but also prominently in the marketplace. The reality is that many nonbelievers spend most of their time in the marketplace, and it may be the primary space where they encounter expressions of God's power.

Being intentional about utilizing your God-given gifts in the marketplace provides a unique opportunity to impact those who may never step foot inside a church building. It's a powerful way to embody God's love, grace, and transformative power in the spaces where people live out their daily lives.

According to 1 Corinthians 12:7-11, we've been given spiritual gifts for the common good of the body, and the Bible doesn't limit these gifts to use only within the church walls or on mission trips. You won't find that in the scriptures.

Ignorance of these truths can be advantageous to Satan. These gifts are meant for our homes, workplaces, and marketplaces like hospitals, the White House, Hollywood, and beyond. Utilizing these gifts outside the church is crucial because Satan, the god of this world, is active in all these areas. To tap into your supernatural potential, it's essential to employ these spiritual gifts everywhere, including the marketplace.

Spiritual gifts are vital in healing in a hospital setting, providing supernatural knowledge to offer hope to a secretary over the phone. These gifts have the power to transform an atmosphere of seemingly impossible negotiations into a victorious turnaround. They can shape your perspective on situations, enabling you to discern the spirit at work in any given circumstance. Ultimately, spiritual gifts make us carriers of the love and power of Christ to the world around us.

Dividing the nine spiritual gifts into three groups can provide a clearer understanding. The three commonly recognized categories are:

Revelatory Gifts:

- Word of Wisdom
- Word of Knowledge
- Discerning of Spirits

Power Gifts:

- Faith
- Miracles
- Gifts of Healings

Vocal Gifts:

- Prophecy
- Tongues
- Interpretation of Tongues

This categorization helps to highlight the different aspects of how the spiritual gifts operate and their distinct roles within the body of believers.

Revelatory Gifts

1. Word of Wisdom

This is the application of the truth of the Word of God. It is knowledge of God's Word and knowing how to apply it to every area of life. The Bible is the Best Success Book ever written! I cannot tell you how many times I've taken the wisdom found in the word of God and applied it to different areas of my life, resulting in consistent success. The practical application of biblical wisdom has proven to be a reliable resource in navigating various aspects of life.

> *"Wisdom is the principal thing, therefore get wisdom and with all thy getting, get understanding."*
>
> *—Proverbs 4:7*

As the Bible emphasizes, wisdom should be a priority in our daily requests—it's everything! It goes beyond just memorizing scriptures; the key is knowing how to apply them. Jesus exemplified the application of wisdom from the word of God when tempted by Satan after emerging from the wilderness. Jesus demonstrated profound wisdom by precisely selecting the appropriate scriptures to counter the temptations that Satan threw at Him. His ability to respond with the right scriptures showcased a deep understanding and mastery of the Word of God. Similarly, we must discern when to assertively apply God's word without hesitation.

Wisdom becomes a guide for decision-making, influencing choices at home, in marriage, and in the workplace. It empowers you to recognize when swift decisions are necessary, preventing unnecessary procrastination on important matters.

I remember when we listed our house for sale, preparing to move to a new state. Despite being on the market for several months, there was no interest from potential buyers. We fervently prayed, but the situation persisted. Then, one Saturday morning, the story of the 12 spies from the Bible dropped into my heart. Remembering how they explored the promised land and brought back a negative report, I immediately read the story aloud to my husband and kids. We sensed the Lord revealing that we were mirroring the doubt of the 12 spies.

Recognizing our unbelief, we quickly repented and earnestly cried out to God for mercy. Miraculously, within three weeks from that moment, our house sold, and we relocated to Georgia. Reflecting on this, I am deeply grateful for the wisdom to apply God's word to our situation, resulting in swift success.

2. Word of Knowledge

It's a supernatural insight granted by the Holy Spirit, revealing information that you couldn't have known without the Spirit's prompting. For instance, imagine encountering someone you've never met, and inexplicably, you gain a sense about them. The Lord begins revealing information, and when you share it, they respond, "How did you know that?"

A similar experience happened to me recently at a prayer gathering. A lady I had never seen before introduced herself, and as I spoke with her, her face seemed oddly familiar. The Lord began imparting insights about her, leading to a profound moment. I shared what I was receiving, and unexpectedly, she started sobbing, undergoing a powerful deliverance that night. She went through a full-on deliverance that night and was completely set free.

This transformative encounter started with a word of knowledge—a gift we should earnestly desire from God. And if you don't know that you have the gift, you'd never use it. Recognizing and using this gift can elevate your leadership to an extraordinary level. Whether in the marketplace, supermarket, classroom or at home, this gift proves invaluable. Every parent should actively seek this gift, as it provides profound insights into potential dynamics within your home involving your children and spouse.

3. Discerning of Spirits

The third revelatory gift is the discerning of spirits, providing insight into the "spirit," motives, or intentions operating behind a situation or individual. It's a supernatural ability to distinguish truth from falsehood, and in the current times we are living in, this gift holds significant importance.

The ability to judge rightly can be crucial for safeguarding your destiny and that of your loved ones. In the marketplace, possessing and using this gift can mean steering clear of potentially fraudulent or disastrous business partnerships. When something or someone appears "off," even if others don't see it, trusting your "gut"(your inner prompting from the Holy Ghost) and seeking guidance from the Holy Spirit is vital to know what is truly operating behind the "smoke screen."

Whether in a church setting or while listening to a so-called "prophet," you are discerning that something is off. It's important not to ignore the promptings because there are so many imposters out there.

Power Gifts

The first gift in the Power Gift category is the gift of Faith. Faith is the cornerstone for all other spiritual gifts, being the key that pleases God. Faith is believing beforehand what will only make sense later.

1. Faith

Faith in the marketplace empowers believers to take dominion and embrace risks they might otherwise avoid. Faith is like a muscle requiring daily exercise for growth and development, achieved through consistently reading God's word. Romans 10:17 emphasizes, "Faith comes by hearing and hearing by the word of God."

To grow in faith, you must know and believe God's word. Individuals with the gift of Faith hold a strong conviction that nothing is impossible for God. They wholeheartedly believe that, with God, all things are possible, devoid of any doubt.

Faith involves risk-taking. It is having a promise and stepping out even if it doesn't make sense. Abraham would have been considered a fool by most Christians in today's world for leaving his father's house. But then the Bible says, "His faith was attributed to him for righteousness."

So when you step out in faith to build your business, when you step out in faith to move your family 600 miles away from their friends only to start all over again in a different state, when you step out and call those things that are not as though they were, it is attributed to you as righteousness.

Faith is not easy, and it is uncomfortable. But there is a reward for faith. Hebrews 11:6 reminds us, "But without faith it is impossible to please Him, for he who comes to God must believe that He is, and that He is a rewarder of those who diligently seek Him."

Entrepreneurs have the gift of faith. Have you stepped out and borrowed money to invest in your mindset and your business? That's faith! Have you sold your house only to use the money to invest in a project? That's the gift of faith, friend.

Maybe you've stepped out in faith to start a business, and you failed forward. Good job, you tried, and it is faith. Faith involves taking risks, calculated risks. It will be attributed to you as righteousness. Remember, there is no faith in what's easy or normal.

The next gift in the category of Power Gifts is the Gift of Miracles.

2. Gift of Miracles

This gift empowers you to perform extraordinary miracles that defy natural explanation, attributed solely to the supernatural work of God. The gift of working miracles is not limited to performing miracles like the blind can now see, the lame person can now walk, the deaf can hear, etc. According to Strong's Concordance, it also means the power and influence that belong to riches and wealth. This means there is a level of influence that God desires for you to Have.

This revelation indicates that the power of miracles is available to you in the marketplace, offering the power to create wealth. In today's context, we require this power to venture into the marketplace, generate wealth, and establish a lasting legacy for our children and grandchildren. Proverbs 13:22 reinforces this idea, "A good man leaves an inheritance to his children's children, but the wealth of the sinner is stored up for the righteous."

3. Gift of Healing

It's a supernatural manifestation of God's power to mend anything that has been broken, whether physically, emotionally, or spiritually. As a child in covenant with your covenant God, you have a right to divine health. It is one of your privileges.

Jesus took upon Himself your sins on the cross, and He also bore your diseases, pain, and sicknesses. Unfortunately, some Christians doubt that this gift is accessible to them in the present day. Often, when you ask whether they believe they can be healed, they respond with phrases like, "If it's God's will …" However, Jesus encourages you to stand on His word, emphasizing "ONLY BELIEVE" in Mark 5:36.

This gift holds power not only within the church but extends to every place you find yourself—the supermarket, on a plane, at work, at home, and beyond. You can bring the supernatural gift of healing to those in desperate need.

I recall an incident from a few years ago when one of my husband's patients experienced a life-threatening situation in the operating room, leading to an ICU admission. After days of no improvement, the doctors were considering discontinuing life support.

My husband shared this case with me, and we earnestly prayed for a miracle. Feeling a burden for the patient, I wondered, "What if she didn't know the Lord?" Our prayers were fervent, and we sought a miracle. My husband went to the hospital's waiting room to pray for family members who had flown in from out of town to bid their farewells.

The next day, a miracle occurred in the ICU. God revived the patient, and she eventually recovered, being discharged after a few days. This miraculous event unfolded not within the confines of a church but at the hospital, in the marketplace, precisely where my husband spends most of his days.

Vocal Gifts

The last part of the spiritual gifts is called "vocal gifts."

1. The Gift of Prophecy

Paul says to earnestly desire this gift (1 Corinthians 14:1, paraphrased). Prophecy involves proclaiming God's intentions and unveiling hidden matters. It grants the ability to perceive what others may not. This gift serves purposes such as exhortation, rebuke, and correction. Prophecy is about revealing the future, and individuals with a prophetic inclination may receive visions and dreams.

If you resonate with these characteristics, you may possess this significant gift. It is valuable within the church and also in the marketplace. Imagine the positive impact on businesses, corporations, and family dynamics if the prophetic gift were active, helping prevent erroneous decisions, unfavorable partnerships, and conflicts. The Bible says to use the gift of prophecy in proportion to your faith. Be sure to ask for a measure of faith and earnestly desire the gift of prophecy.

2. The Gift of Tongues (and Interpretation)

This differs from your prayer language. When you speak in tongues, you speak directly to God, bypassing all human reasoning. He who speaks in an unknown tongue does not speak to man but speaks to God.

However, the gift of tongues and interpretation is the ability to speak out a message from God in a heavenly tongue. Someone with a gift of interpretation has the supernatural ability to translate the message into a language you can understand. Some folks don't believe this, but it is still in your Bible.

These gifts are given to us by the Spirit. These are not what we use for our own selfish gains but for the edification of the body and for the glory of God. These gifts, when activated both inside and outside the four walls of the church, can be a powerful tool. They can help you become successful in all areas of your life.

HAVE YOU BURIED YOUR GIFTS?

*"He who is faithful in what is least is
faithful also in much."*

—Luke 16:10

You have one or more gifts given to you by God. These gifts come with a purpose, an assignment on earth that God intends for you to fulfill using your unique abilities. You don't have to rely on others to acknowledge your gifts; instead, directly seek guidance from God to reveal the talents He has placed within you.

Let me ask you a question. Have you hidden your gifts and talents because of rejection? Have you buried your gifts because of fear of men? You can't hide from God. He sure will chase after you because whatever gifts and talents He has given you, He requires that you grow them.

Have you hidden your gifts because of doubts? This was me. I doubted I could be used for anything significant, so I never really developed my gifts. I was just like the man in the biblical story of the Parable of Talents. The master gave the servant five talents; he went out and doubled it. The next one he gave two talents; he also went out and doubled it. The last servant, he gave one talent. The man told his master that he did not go out there to double his talent because he was afraid, so he buried the one talent that was given to him. This was me for many years. I buried my gift because I was wounded. I had so many doubts, and I was afraid.

Do you have gifts for designing things, and you belittle it? Is this you? "You are so good at encouraging others." And you respond, "Oh, it's nothing." "It's no biggie."

Whatever gift He has given you, He wants you to grow it. You have been given these gifts and talents for a purpose. Are you good with teaching others the things you know? He wants you to grow it. Are you good with working with your hands as a craftsman? The Lord wants you to grow it.

Whatever gifts you have, He gave them to you. Don't be like the third servant in the story above who hid his talent because he did not see its value. Don't undervalue what you've been given. God views not using your talent as wickedness and laziness. You are meant to invest, double, and make a profit from what God has deposited in you. The other two men took the talents that were given to them, doubled them, and made a profit. God deserves a reward for whatever He has deposited inside of you. Agree with God quickly, then uncover and discover your gifts and talents.

When you are faithful with the little, He promises to make you ruler over much. It's time to stop comparing your talent to sister Suzie's on the other side of the block. Keep your eyes fixed on the giver of the gift. Be grateful for your unique gifts, go out there, and give it your best effort. You were made to grow and multiply your gifts.

Take initiative to use these gifts not only within the church but also at home, on the street, in the marketplace, at your gym, or wherever you find yourself. Trust in the Lord with all Your heart; do not lean on your own understanding and He will direct your steps. If someone like me, who grew up most of my life being rejected, could rise above it, so can you!

Many people merely admire the beautifully wrapped box filled with gifts God gave them, never taking the initiative to open them and uncover the treasures within. This is similar to the striped caterpillar humbly crawling along the milk-weed plant's stem. To uncover its inherent power, potential, and purpose, the caterpillar must transform, breaking free from the cocoon to emerge as a majestic butterfly soaring high in the air.

Like the butterfly stepping out of its comfort zone to liberate its shimmering auburn wings, it's your turn to explore your unique gifts. Break free from limiting beliefs, fears, and doubts to discover your wings so that you can fly to new heights.

When you neglect to open your box of gifts, not only do you miss out on boundless opportunities, but the lives of others are also deprived of experiencing the unique contributions only you can offer. It's time to discover your untapped potential, ready to be unleashed.

TAKE YOUR POSITION

"You will not need to fight in this battle. Position yourselves, stand still and see the salvation of the LORD, who is with you, O Judah and Jerusalem!"

—2 Chronicles 20:17

When the Lord spoke to me through His Word, saying, "Take your position," I initially had little understanding of what that meant, except that I needed to anchor myself in His Word.

Through nearly three years, His gracious leading gradually unveiled what it truly meant to "take your position." Simply put, "take your position" signifies standing firmly in your delegated authority and designated place while confronting your adversaries. Our rightful place is the position Christ secured for us on the cross, where His blood grants us access to the status of a son or daughter. It's a position of authority where fear holds no sway. Empowered by the strength of the Almighty God and the anointing of the Holy Spirit, we fearlessly and boldly confront anything that seeks to hinder our journey, purpose, or God's calling on our lives.

Let's examine from the Bible men and women of God who stepped into their God-given positions to fulfill the purpose that God had ordained for their lives.

In the Bible, a man boldly took his position even when he faced dire circumstances. Nehemiah, the cupbearer for King Artaxerxes, received news that the walls and gates of Jerusalem lay in ruins, destroyed by fire. With unwavering determination, he approached the king to request permission to return to Jerusalem and rebuild. Nehemiah fervently prayed for a breakthrough, and the Lord granted him favor with the king. His prayer in Nehemiah 1:5-10 is truly powerful and worth reading in your own time.

Upon returning to Jerusalem, Nehemiah commenced the task of rebuilding the walls. Amid this great work, he faced ridicule and mockery from two men, Sanballat and Tobiah. The Bible tells us Nehemiah prayed to Elohim and posted guards day and night, becoming a vigilant watchman in prayer (Nehemiah 4:9). He was a man who knew how to fight while he built.

Despite manipulation and intimidation, God strengthened Nehemiah, and the walls were successfully rebuilt. The Lord rendered his enemies' counsel ineffective. Just like I, too, have experienced a situation where legal counsel, or lawyers, posed threats and intimidation, claiming I was responsible for extensive legal fees. This could have amounted to substantial costs. However, God intervened, turning their counsel into nothing, just as He did for Nehemiah. It's a powerful testament to the principle of "take your position."

Deborah exemplified a woman who fully understood her power and authority. At a time when Jabin, the King of Canaan, had oppressed the Israelites for two decades, the Lord entrusted her with a message. He directed Deborah, a prophetess, to convey His instructions to Barak regarding a battle against Jabin and his commander, Sisera. The Lord promised to deliver Sisera into Barak's hands.

However, Barak hesitated to engage in this battle alone, so he requested Deborah's presence. In response, Deborah conveyed a prophecy that if she accompanied him, the Lord would deliver Sisera into the hands of a woman. Despite this, Deborah took her position and went with Barak into battle. True to the prophecy, the Lord granted victory through the hands of a woman named Jael.

Deborah's decision to take her position led to a victory facilitated by divine wisdom. Jael was supernaturally guided to defeat God's enemy. When we also take our position, the Lord bestows upon us the wisdom and insight to approach our challenges in a way that subdues the enemy without them even realizing it.

There are times when taking your position requires a period of preparation. The story of Esther serves as a powerful example of this need for preparation. After being adopted by her uncle Mordecai after her parents' passing, Esther underwent a process of readiness.

Among many young women, Esther was chosen to undergo beauty treatments in the palace for a whole year. The purpose was to select the next queen to replace Vashti. Esther's exceptional favor led to her being chosen as the queen. Most of us are familiar with this story.

It takes a significant turn when a man named Haman plots to destroy the Jewish people. Mordecai implores Esther to take her position and approach the king to address this dire matter. Esther, in response, calls for a three-day fast to muster the courage to stand before the king. Her bravery pays off, and the king grants her request, effectively saving her entire nation.

This captivating story imparts valuable lessons for us to glean from. Just as Esther needed preparation to assume her role, there are moments when we, too, require divine preparation. Esther's purification process, symbolized by the use of oils, represents God's cleansing, purifying, and transformative work in our lives. Through the blood of Christ, He leads us through a journey of repentance and sanctification. As God's oil of acceptance washes off residues of rejection and abandonment, then all of the comparison, competition, and identity issues we've carried for so long begin to fade away.

While the preparation for assuming your rightful position may seem like a delay or setback, rest assured it's precisely what you need to become battle-ready. This very process equips you to step into the King's court, bringing about breakthroughs in your marriage, finances, relationships, and health.

It's the very thing you need to potentially bring salvation to a "nation." Stepping into your delegated authority is crucial, requiring submission, consecration, and devotion to God. Failure to embrace your rightful position can lead to suffering for your children and jeopardize your family's well-being.

Overcoming obstacles like fear, unbelief, self-doubt, limiting beliefs, disobedience, and frustration is essential to assuming these roles.

Unfortunately, defiance and a lack of cooperation with God can significantly delay your destiny, affecting your family, lineage, and even nations. Beyond your personal journey, there are so many precious lives waiting for help on the other side of your obedience—lives connected to you that you are called to lead to freedom. It's time to get into your position.

Let's look at one final example of a young man who stepped into his position confidently and without hesitation.

FACING YOUR GIANT

"I will not be afraid of ten thousands of people Who have set themselves against me all around."

—Psalm 3:6

Let's revisit one of my favorite Bible stories, one that has left a profound impact on me since my childhood. I've drawn valuable insights from it and am eager to share it with you. It's the timeless story of David and Goliath. You might already be familiar with this powerful showdown. David's character is truly fascinating in this narrative. He's not a flawless hero but a man with his own share of imperfections. He committed adultery and murder, which might surprise you, given that he was considered "the apple of God's eye." It's a thought-provoking aspect of the story, isn't it? It challenges the notion that one must be perfect for God to use them.

That's a belief I held growing up, but here's the good news: only one is truly perfect, and He was crucified for us. Jesus didn't give His life so that we could attain perfection. Yes, He desires that we walk in holiness before Him, but expecting perfection from us? That's a far cry from the truth. The Bible is loaded with examples of how God used imperfect individuals to accomplish His plans here on Earth.

Now, let's delve deeper into this cherished story of mine. I hold it dear because it's a powerful story of courage, faith, and the ultimate victory of the underdog. Picture David, the youngest in his family. When the Lord sent the prophet Samuel to Bethlehem to anoint a new king from among the eight sons of Jesse, the assumption was that the eldest son would be the chosen one.

But as we're reminded in 1 Samuel 16:7, "... for man looks at the outward appearance, but the LORD looks at the heart." David stood out because his heart was devoted to God. That's why he was selected over his brothers.

This story speaks to the core of what truly matters to God: the state of our hearts. It's a reminder that God's choices often defy societal expectations, showing us that it's our faith and character that He values most. This story inspires and encourages me, and I hope it does the same for you.

This extraordinary story unfolds during a conflict between the Israelites and the Philistines. The Philistines, led by a fearsome giant named Goliath, challenged the Israelites to send out a champion for a one-on-one battle.

Now, picture a young shepherd boy named David. He's the youngest in his family, armed not with heavy armor but with unwavering faith. David steps forward to face the giant, Goliath. He carries just a sling and a few smooth stones. David was a shepherd boy. Where in the world did he get the courage to step up and face this giant? David reported that when a lion and a bear came and carried off the sheep from the flock, he went after the bear and the lion. David struck them and rescued his sheep from their grip. David said: "Your servant has killed both a bear and a lion. So this uncircumcised Philistine will be just like one of them." He boldly proclaimed that the same God that delivered him from the mouth of the lion and the bear is the same God that will deliver him from this giant!

As the two adversaries meet, the tension in the air is palpable. David's heart pounds, but his resolve doesn't waver. David said to Goliath, "You come against me with the sword and spear and a javelin, but I come against you in the name of the Almighty, God of the armies of Israel, whom you have defiled. This day, the Lord will hand you over to me, and I will give the carcasses of the Philistine army to the birds of the air and the beasts of the earth, and the whole world will know that there is a God in Israel."

Do you see what is happening here? Are you facing a giant in your family? Do you have a giant sickness? What is the giant coming against you right now? Fill in the blank. Is it your marriage? Your finances? That business that you would like to start but are too scared to take the next step for? Facing a giant of fear? Where is your resolve? Where is your fight?

David literally says, "C'mon—I know my God will fight for me; therefore, I will not back down from this uncircumcised Philistine." Are you facing a "giant"? Are you focused on the giant of fear you are facing, or are you looking to the Almighty God who cannot lose a battle?

You cannot allow your current situation to determine your future. You cannot allow the "giant" you are facing to determine your level of faith. David was so confident in His God that he was willing to take the risk. Don't allow your circumstances or intimidation to stop you from pursuing your dreams.

With a stone in his sling, David takes aim and hurls it at the massive Goliath. The stone, guided by David's unwavering faith, finds its mark, striking Goliath squarely in the forehead. The giant, once so imposing, comes crashing down.

Just as Goliath fell before David's courage and faith, your giants will also crumble, whatever they may be. Are you facing the giant of excuses, the impostor syndrome, or the giant of limiting beliefs? It doesn't matter what form your giant takes. To succeed in any endeavor, we all must confront our giants. With the Almighty God by your side and the power of the Holy Spirit, that giant is destined to fall.

Remember, the Bible reminds us that "nothing shall be impossible for those who believe." It doesn't say, "Nothing, except for marriage, finances, or health." It boldly proclaims that nothing shall be impossible. So, just as David's faith toppled Goliath, let your faith conquer your giants and pave the way for your success. Your faith is your greatest ally in the face of any giant in your path.

David's fearless attack on Goliath was a sight to behold. He was confident that the same God who had rescued him from the clutches of lions and bears would also deliver him from this intimidating giant. In the face of any challenge, you too must charge forward without hesitation, head to head with whatever stands in your way, and decisively cut off the head of your personal "Goliath." It's about taking the necessary steps toward your goals, whether it's learning a new skill, embarking on a weight loss journey, or pursuing any desired outcome.

Just like David's unwavering trust in God, trust plays a pivotal role in achieving success. It's a significant part of winning in the game of life. The Bible wisely reminds us that "he who trusts in the Lord shall prosper." You were created to make an impact on this Earth. Deep within you lies incredible gifts and talents waiting to be awakened. It's time to become the person God has destined you to be so you can fulfill the purpose He has for you and, in turn, leave a lasting legacy that impacts the lives assigned to you for generations to come.

So, take action, do something, and become someone with a profound influence. Your journey to success starts with unwavering faith and trust, just like David's, in the Almighty God.

God's plan for each of us is unique, and we are chosen, set apart, and filled with His Holy Spirit to accomplish everything He has destined for us. Our choices along the way play a significant role in realizing that plan.

I've applied these very strategies in all areas of my life. Whether in my marriage, business, or relationships, these are the principles I've relied on to attain the success I enjoy today.

God has a plan for you! You have been chosen, set apart, and filled with His Holy Spirit to achieve everything he has destined for you. You have a choice to make. You were designed by the Creator to excel in your assigned area of influence.

FINDING HIDDEN GEMS IN YOUR PAIN, TRIALS, AND DISAPPOINTMENTS

"And we know that all things work together for good to those who love God, to those who are the called according to His purpose."

—Romans 8:28

I've saved the best for last—this next insight is your key to moving from confusion to clarity, from struggle to strength, and from broken to bold. We've all faced various challenges in life, but recognizing that you are more than the circumstances you've encountered is a game changer.

For instance, being born into poverty doesn't dictate that you'll live and die in poverty. You will always find individuals who've overcome adversity because they made a choice to let go. They made a choice to stop being a victim. Knowing your identity and understanding who you are shifts you from being a victim of circumstances to embracing a victor's mindset.

If anyone had the right to be a victim, Joseph would be a prime example.

Let's take a deeper look at this inspiring story.

As mentioned in the introduction, Joseph held a special place in his father Jacob's heart, being his favorite son. To symbolize this affection, Jacob gifted Joseph a vibrant coat of many colors. Intriguingly, Joseph had dreams of his family bowing down to him, which he openly shared with his brothers. Regrettably, this revelation stirred jealousy among them, ultimately leading to a plan to get rid of Joseph.

His brothers threw Joseph into a pit and sold him as a slave to passing merchants. Talk about sibling rivalry gone wrong! Joseph ended up in Egypt, serving in the house of Potiphar, an officer of Pharaoh. Things seemed to be on the up, but then came another twist—he was falsely accused of attempting to seduce Potiphar's wife and ended up in prison.

Now, prisons back then weren't exactly fun places, but Joseph's gift of interpreting dreams caught the attention of Pharaoh's cupbearer. This connection turned out to be a game changer. Pharaoh himself had some puzzling dreams, and Joseph was the man with the plan to decode them.

His interpretation? Joseph used one of the gifts given to him by God to interpret the dream: seven years of abundance followed by seven years of famine. Impressed, Pharaoh appointed Joseph as the second-in-command to manage food storage during the years of plenty. Here, we witness how he applied his gift of wisdom ingeniously. He devised a brilliant plan to store food for seven years, ensuring his people would not succumb to starvation.

Fast forward to the famine, and Joseph's brothers, who were hit hard, traveled to Egypt seeking food. They didn't recognize Joseph, but he sure knew them. After some dramatic encounters and tests, Joseph revealed his identity. There were tears, hugs, and a family reunion in Egypt.

Joseph forgave his brothers, and the whole clan moved to Egypt, where they settled and prospered. The guy who was once sold into slavery ended up saving not only Egypt but also his family. It's a story of resilience, forgiveness, and the unexpected journey from the pit to the palace.

After Joseph rose to power in Egypt and reconciled with his family, he got married and had two sons. Their names and meanings added another layer to the story.

Joseph named his firstborn son Manasseh, saying, "For God has made me forget all my afflictions and all my father's house." The name Manasseh reflects Joseph's gratitude for the fresh start he found in Egypt, allowing him to move from trial into triumph. The second son was named Ephraim, and Joseph explained, "For God has caused me to be fruitful in the land of my affliction" (Genesis 41:51-52, paraphrased). Ephraim's name symbolizes the prosperity and blessings that Joseph experienced despite the challenging circumstances he had faced in Egypt.

Proverbs 14:23a says, "In all labor, there is profit." The word "labor" means work, but it also means toil, pain, sorrow, and hardships. So, the Bible literally tells you there is profit in your hardships.

What if I told you that your life experiences have value? All the experiences you have had—the good, the bad, and the ugly—all have significant value. Joseph chose to find and see the hidden gems in his pain. When he finally revealed himself to his brothers in Genesis 45:5, He said, "... For God sent me before you to preserve life." He chose to see the hidden gems in his troubles.

Just like Joseph, you, too, must decide that despite all of the trauma, pain, and troubles that you have gone through, you will not allow your circumstances to determine your future.

I believe there are two factors that can shape our view of the experiences we have had in life and what we choose to do with them. We can choose to be a victim of our circumstances or become a victor. These two factors are worth taking a look at.

External factors: all the things that happened to you, all the things outside of you that you had no control of. For example, if you were born with a defect, you were abused, raped, or got into an accident and became paralyzed, or you were brought up in a poor situation that caused you to be broken.

Internal factors: all the things inside of you. All the gifts and talents that were placed inside of you by the great, creative Father. Most people think that external factors determine what their future will look like. But, may I present to you that your internal factors are actually what determines what your future will look like. There is a seed of creativity that God himself has put inside each and every one of us, just like a fruit has a seed inside of it. That fruit has everything it needs to reproduce and grow.

In the same way, God has placed His seed of creativity inside of us. This allows us to become fruitful as He commands in Genesis 1:28. We are to fill the earth and then subdue it. In other words, anytime you decide to move in the direction of what God is calling you to do, disruptions will come along as well. So you are to trample upon anything that tries to stop you from fulfilling your destiny. God caused Joseph to become fruitful in the land of his affliction, in the area of his sufferings, pain, and trauma. More often than not, when you have gone through afflictions, you have a different kind of fruitfulness that you most likely would not have had if you had not gone through that trouble. In the midst of life's toughest trials, you discover your true self. Showing up even when it's tough reveals your inner strength and character. This is where character and grit are built—a defining moment, a choice between caving in or facing the challenge with faith, boldness, and a firm trust in God.

There are hidden gems in your pain and your sufferings. The afflictions Joseph went through prepared him for the assignment for which he was created. If Joseph had not been in Egypt, who would have interpreted the dream for Pharaoh? If Joseph had not been in Egypt, who would have come up with the brilliant plan to save the nations from starvation?

I want to encourage you to learn how to discover the treasured gems hidden in your life, even in the brokenness, pain, and trauma you may have experienced. Finding these hidden gems changed my perspective and turned my hopelessness into hope.

I was born and raised in Nigeria and lived with my father, along with my siblings, in a very poor and abusive condition. I watched all kinds of wickedness, evil, and witchcraft being done to us as a child. We had no mom around to help and protect us. I was sexually abused without my father even knowing. My father hated my guts. I know what it feels like to not have food to eat. Our shoes had holes in them because we were very poor; even the other poor people called us "poor." I have had my share of physical and verbal abuse. I was often called "stupid" instead of referring to me by my name. Somewhere in all of the troubles, I had lost my identity. I share this part of my story because, like Joseph, I, too, have had my share of pain, trauma, and afflictions.

One day, I learned to find the hidden treasures in my pain. I realized that everything that happened to me actually happened for me. It was a setup for my destiny.

Trials and pain often produce heat and pressure, but at the same time, they can turn your darkest moments into something beautiful like a diamond. Similar to how diamonds form under intense pressure, your inner strength and brilliance often emerge through the struggles you face. Just as a sculptor molds a masterpiece from a block of stone through meticulous chiseling, your character takes shape and becomes refined through the trials you endure. Remember, just as storms precede rainbows, and the darkest nights give way to the brightest mornings, your most challenging moments pave the way for your greatest achievements.

James 1: 2-4 says, "My brethren, count it all joy when you fall into various trials, knowing that the testing of your faith produces patience. But let patience have *its* perfect work, that you may be perfect and complete, lacking nothing."

During a challenging period when progress seemed impossible, I was caught in a whirlwind of pain, trauma, anger, and unforgiveness.

However, the Lord guided me to discover hidden gems within those experiences. Much to my surprise, I uncovered numerous "diamonds" in the midst of my afflictions. The transforming power of these discoveries has not only impacted my life but has also been evident in the lives of those I've coached and counseled.

Here are a few of the positive outcomes from my pain and trauma:

- Growing up in adversity fueled a deep compassion for the poor within me. I am passionate about taking care of them, and I've been blessed with a business that allows me to support those in need by ensuring no one goes without basic necessities.
- The hardships brought me closer to God, making Him my anchor during difficult times.
- My past experiences have equipped me for my current role as a coach. I help others overcome challenges, providing guidance and imparting skills for success in relationship and wealth creation.

The ability to find hidden gems in every trial not only fosters gratitude but also facilitates forgiveness toward those who may have caused pain.

Joseph serves as an inspiring example of someone who discovered hidden gems in his trials. The names of his two children, Manasseh and Ephraim, stand as living reminders of God's faithfulness and the transformative power of forgiveness and resilience.

Similar to Joseph's ability to discover hidden gems in his trials, we, too, need to undertake the same journey to transition from anger and disappointment to joy and freedom. It's time to move away from a victim mindset into a victor mentality because there is no advancement without adversity. And there is no strength without struggle.

What would happen if you start being grateful for things you have been bitter about? What would happen if you discovered that everything that happened to you was a setup and preparation for your assignment? Rise up and learn how to tell your story because there is a world out there waiting to hear the story of how you turned your burdens into blessings.

Here are the steps to take when you're ready to discover the hidden gems in your pain.

- Create a list of the trials and pain you have experienced, ranging from recent events to childhood memories.
- For each trial, jot down the positive changes or hidden gems you've experienced as a result. This could include shifts in attitude, changes in the direction of your life, knowledge gained, and more.
- Sit down with the Holy Spirit and ask Him to help you "gem hunt" through each painful experience you've

had. You'd be surprised what He reveals to you, gems that you might have overlooked.

- Take a moment to pray, express gratitude to God for each positive experience or hidden gem, and thank Him for the trials.

- Keep a gratitude journal by your bedside. Each night, before you go to bed, write down five things you are grateful for about that day.

Gratitude is one of the keys to success.

Completing this exercise will most likely make forgiveness easier. Like Joseph, you will soon find yourself saying, "God has made me forget my afflictions, and God has made me fruitful in the area of my affliction."

Now, go and uncover those gems and see how your challenges can transform you into a champion.

A THREE-DAY PRAYER AND FASTING GUIDE

This section is a Free Bonus that contains guidance for a three-day prayer and fasting schedule.

Each day has a prayer focus and some scripture suggestions.

This is only a guide. Always follow the guidance and the leading of the Holy Spirit.

First, let me clarify this: Biblical Fasting is abstaining from food for a certain period of time. It's NOT a social media fast, nor is it fasting from certain foods like chocolate, sugar, etc. Those are called dietary changes. This is a biblical fast, similar to the type of fast Queen Esther did in Esther 4:16. The only difference is that we abstain from food but not water. OK! I want to make sure I'm clear on this.

Fasting in itself is not the answer. Jesus is the answer! However, fasting helps us to humble ourselves before the almighty God. According to Isaiah 58, there are several benefits to fasting.

Fasting Breaks Oppression

With fasting, your light shall break forth. The word "light" in Hebrew means the light of instructions, the light of prosperity. It allows you to gain clear direction where things have been obscure in your life. You'll now be able to hear and see unambiguously.

The Lord will guide you continually. He will satisfy your soul (will, mind, and emotions) in drought. Where you have been in a dry and weary place, God says He will water your soul, and you will be like a watered garden and a spring of fresh water. Fresh renewing of your mind, where rivers of living waters flow out of your innermost being. Fasting will empower you to raise up the faulty foundation, and you'll be a repairer of the breach.

Finally, fasting brings your answers speedily. Isaiah 58:9 says: "Then you shall call, and the LORD will answer; You shall cry, and He will say, 'Here I am.' If you take away the yoke from your midst, the pointing of the finger, and speaking vanity." I looked up the word "vanity" in Hebrew—it means trouble, wickedness, sorrow, and idolatry. Do not let any wicked words, idolatry words, lies, etc., come out of your mouth. You have the power of life and death in your mouth. I will encourage you to read Isaiah 58 in its entirety to familiarize yourself with the benefits of fasting.

Day One: Repent, Repent, Repent

Let's be clear about what repentance is not. It is not crying hysterically and/or feeling sorry for yourself. Nah! It's not a false apology without any kind of changed behavior. Sometimes, you and I can quickly blurt out the word "sorry" to take the issue off the table. But if we are being honest, we are not really sorry. Or perhaps we are only sorry that we got caught?

True repentance means to turn away from your sin.

The Greek definition for repentance is a change of mind, as it appears to one who repents of something he has done. Repentance requires you to make a decision and, in turn, have a change of mind, resulting in a changed behavior.

Repentance is an invitation from God. It's His mercy that draws you to repentance. You need the ministry of the Holy Spirit to completely turn away from your sins. Ask Him to help you turn away from your sin.

> *"I tell you, no; but unless you repent you will all likewise perish" (Luke 13:3).*

> *"And he went into all the region around the Jordan, preaching a baptism of repentance for the remission of sins" (Luke 3:3).*

> *"... The time is fulfilled, and the kingdom of God is at hand. Repent, and believe in the gospel" (Mark 1:15).*

> *"And whenever you stand praying, if you have anything against anyone, forgive him, that your Father in heaven may also forgive you your trespasses" (Mark 11:25).*

Guidelines For Prayer

Father, in the name of Jesus, I humble myself before you. Thank you for your mercy triumphs over judgment. I ask for forgiveness for the sins that I have committed against you. Thank you that according to Proverbs 28:13, no one who conceals transgressions will prosper, but one who confesses and forsakes them will obtain mercy. I am confessing sins before you today. I repent for the sins of idolatry. Because anything I love more than my obedience to your word is idolatry. I have looked to other things to fill me up. I repent for calling what is evil good and what is good evil. I repent for idolizing people, celebrities, pastors, social media influencers, prophets, etc. I repent for not taking your word as my life's final word of authority and truth. I repent for not trusting you and allowing the enemy to plant seeds of doubt in my mind. I repent for playing small because I don't understand the power that lives inside of me. I repent for the times you spoke to me about certain things, but I doubted my ability to hear, so I ignored it and disobeyed your instructions.

Father, I repent for bowing down to the spirit of fear and intimidation from the enemy. I repent for walking in the counsel of the ungodly and standing in the way of sinners. I repent for entertaining and allowing filthy words and crude jokes to come out of my mouth. I repent for not guarding my ear and eye gates, allowing filth to come through my eyes and ears.

I repent for the sin of comparison that I have allowed to steal my joy. I repent for being distracted when I was supposed to be busy doing the things you asked me to do. I repent for being the chief excuse maker. I repent for (list all your sins here—gossip, lying, laziness, pride, devising wicked imagination, unforgiveness, bitterness, jealousy, practicing yoga, dabbling in occult things like horoscopes, palm reading, tarot cards, Halloween … fill in the blank).

The following things will hinder your prayers from being answered, so be sure to examine your heart and ask the Holy Spirit to reveal everything that's hidden.

Pride—God hates pride. He will resist the proud. The last thing you need is for God to put His hands out and push yours back. Trust me, you do not want that for your life. Offense and unforgiveness will hinder your prayers!

Let me talk to you about forgiveness. Forgiveness does not mean that what the other person did to you is ok. Forgiveness is for your freedom. Whatever the person has done to you has kept you in prison this far; you don't want unforgiveness to keep you locked up in "prison." You need to forgive so that you can lose yourself from the shackles. Unforgiveness will cause the root of bitterness to spring up in your soul.

Unforgiveness will hinder your prayers from being answered. Read Matthew 18:21-35.

Hebrews 12:15 says, "Looking carefully lest anyone fall short of the grace of God; lest any root of bitterness springing up cause trouble, and by this, many become defiled."

Bitterness and unforgiveness age you. It makes you look ugly. You'll look at yourself in the mirror and hate the person you have become.

It goes down to the cellular level and drips poison on you. Others around you will become contaminated because of the root of bitterness. A parent who has not dealt with bitterness can cause their children to be angry. You can't receive love and cannot release it. Bitterness can cause physical pain, fatigue, anxiety, depression, arthritis, sleep disorders, and inflammation in your body. It will literally defile your relationships, finances, and health.

Unforgiveness clogs the drain. It delays and postpones your destiny.

It would be unfair and out of character for Jesus to reward disobedience. It is against His principles. It's time to stop carrying a burden that He will gladly carry if you will let Him.

One more thing I'd like to share about bitterness: Being critical and judgmental will also cause bitterness. You become what you judge. If you feel like you've been feeling rejected by people lately, check your heart. Ask the Holy Spirit to reveal to you where you have been judgmental.

It's time to cut off the root of bitterness and unforgiveness so you can be free.

Father, forgive us, create in us a clean heart, and renew a right spirit in us. Forgive us for whining, complaining, and refusing to remember where you brought us from. Forgive us for holding onto grudges and taking offense where we should let go. Father, I forgive [add the person or persons name here] for [name whatever they have done to you here]. Forgive people who have left you, walked away from you, abandoned, rejected, cursed, abused, used, and failed you. Forgive the one that raped you. Forgive the one that beat you and left you wounded. Forgive your mom and dad for not being there for you. And forgive yourself!

Release them from your mind, your soul, and your emotions. Forgive them so that you, too, can be forgiven.

Now, once you have forgiven the ones that hurt you, you can break every legal right the demons had over you for not forgiving. Demons love when we harbor unforgiveness. This is how they gain access to you. To close the doors to those demons, you repent, release, break every legal right, and then cast them out.

Ask God to heal you and every part of your life that has been affected as a result of bitterness and unforgiveness. Ask God to heal your fragmented soul and restore your soul like David said in Psalm 23.

Ask Him to uproot any and all the trees that have grown wild as a result of harboring bitterness (Matthew 3:10).

You can boldly apply the blood of Jesus over every area of your life. Go walk in freedom!

Say this, "I forgive them now, I release them, I bless them, and they owe me nothing. I pray that you will show them your mercy, Lord.

"And now, Lord, I choose to forgive myself. I release myself from the burden of guilt and shame, and I lay it at your feet. Wash me with your blood, Father, and cleanse me from all the filth that I have harbored in my heart.

"By faith, I receive the forgiveness you purchased for me on the cross. Your words say you have blotted out the handwriting of decrees against me, and you took them out of the way and nailed them to the cross.

I decree and declare, I am forgiven!"

Day Two: Generational Iniquities/Word Curses

> *"Keeping mercy for thousands, forgiving iniquity and transgression and sin, by no means clearing the guilty, visiting the iniquity of the fathers upon the children and the children's children to the third and the fourth generation"*
> *(Exodus 34:7).*

> *"You shall have no other gods before Me. You shall not make for yourself a carved image—any likeness of anything that is in heaven above, or that is in the earth beneath, or that is in the water under the earth; you shall not bow down to them nor serve them. For I, the LORD your God, am a jealous God, visiting the iniquity of the fathers upon the children to the third and fourth generations of those who hate Me"*
> *(Exodus 20:3-5).*

> *"If the foundations be destroyed, what can a righteous do?"*
> *(Psalm 11:3).*

These verses are just a few among many that show the emphasis God placed on heritage. Most Christians don't believe that curses still exist, and this is the very thing Satan doesn't want you to know. Our ignorance puts us in a very vulnerable position because we cannot fight what we don't know exists. Satan thrives on our ignorance, and so we must do all we can to study this in the scriptures.

Contrary to the beliefs out there—there is something called "generational curse." Curses can be inherited and passed down from one generation to the next.

In simple terms, generational iniquity means that there are some things that your ancestors have done in the past, usually with idolatry. The consequences of this sin are still wreaking havoc in your life. In Mark 9:29, this "kind" in Greek means genos. It means kindred, family, tribe, nation, nationality, descent.

There are many Christians who experience certain delays within their family, and they may be unaware that evil altars or covenants cause them. If you've noticed patterns of delay in your family, maybe it's time to go to the root of the problem rather than dealing with the fruit.

God is not holding you responsible for the sins of your ancestors. Nevertheless, the consequences of these sins can still wreak havoc in someone's life without them knowing. This is clearly illustrated in Leviticus 26:38-39 (paraphrased): "Ye shall perish among the nations, and the land of your enemies shall eat you up. And those of you who are left shall pine away in their iniquity in your enemies' lands; also in their fathers' iniquities, which are with them, they shall pine away."

"Pine away" means to rot away, to decay away, to waste away. If you think about it, how many people are rotting away in the iniquities of their ancestors? I believe so many Christians are wasting away in the iniquities of their fathers because of a lack of knowledge and understanding.

Consider this story in Genesis 11, where Terah, Abraham's father, an idolater, had his son at 70. The generations before him had a record of having their kids at a much younger age, between 29-35. But Terah had a delay. Abraham seemed to have inherited this delay, even though he was a friend of God. His wife, Sarah, married into this and did not give birth until later on in life. Then, Isaac was barren for about 20 years before Rebekah had Jacob and Esau. Jacob had delays as well, as he was a master deceiver. His sons deceived him and sold their brother into slavery.

You notice the patterns of delay and deception in this family. Joshua 24:2 says that Terah, Abraham's father, was an idol worshiper. God hates idolatry, and the consequences of the sin of idolatry brought the delay in the family line. Terah's name also means "delay." Kinda crazy, right?

Sit down with the Holy Spirit and ask Him if there are patterns in your family line you need to know about—things in the past or currently in your life that might be contributing to delays in your bloodline.

For example, patterns where many in the family die of the same disease as CA. Patterns of poverty, bad luck, freak accidents, divorce, delay in marriage, etc. Look for patterns of delay in your life, family history, etc.

Once you identify these things—repent, renounce, break the curses, denounce them, and divorce yourself from them all.

Most Christians ignore the oaths they made to their sorori-
ties, fraternities, and any kind of organizations they joined
that required them to make a covenant. Ask the Holy Spirit
to reveal to you whatever has been hidden. He will bring it to
light (Mark 4:22).

Jesus promised you that the Holy Spirit will lead you into all
truths. He will bring to mind those things you may have forgotten and put on the "back burner" of your mind. Ask the Holy
Spirit to reveal to you if there are any active curses in your life.

Here are some examples of things that could contribute to
existing curses in the life of a believer:

Bringing cursed objects into your home—pay attention to
figurines, children's toys, children's books, decorative items,
paintings, and souvenirs. Also, beware of items and gifts you
bring back home from traveling to other countries. Some of
these items may have been cursed. This is not an unusual
thing in other countries. I was born in Nigeria, so I know this
firsthand.

"Nor shall you bring an abomination into your house, lest
you be doomed to destruction like it. You shall utterly detest
it and utterly abhor it, for it is an accursed thing" (Deuter-
onomy 7:26).

Thank God we have a solution as Christians. Christ died on
the cross and shed His precious blood to pay the price for our
sins. But specifically, the blood of Jesus is the only thing that
can break a covenant that has been set in place by a sin that
was committed by someone in your bloodline.

For example, if someone in your bloodline had an abortion in the past, they have sacrificed to the god of Molech, a false god that demanded the sacrifice of children. This curse would need to be broken off from your life. Why? This can cause things to abort prematurely in your life. Delay in marriage, aborted opportunities, finances, and businesses, etc.

The Bible lays out the principles of how to go about breaking these cycles in your life.

"But if they confess their iniquity and the iniquity of their fathers, with their unfaithfulness in which they were unfaithful to Me, and that they also have walked contrary to Me, and that I also have walked contrary to them and have brought them into the land of their enemies; if their uncircumcised hearts are humbled, and they accept their guilt—then I will remember My covenant with Jacob, and My covenant with Isaac and My covenant with Abraham will I remember; I will remember the land" (Leviticus 26:40-42).

"Blotting out the handwriting of ordinances that was against us, which was contrary to us. And He has taken it out of the way, having nailed it to his cross (Colossians 2:14, paraphrased).

The "ordinances" (the decrees, the contracts that were set in motion because of the sins that were committed). Jesus blotted it all out with His precious blood. Hallelujah!

The blood of Jesus is powerful, but we must appropriate it. We must apply the blood of Jesus over everything pertaining to us. Just like the Lord told His people in the Old Testament to dip Hyssop in the blood and apply it to their doorposts, we, too, must apply the blood. Don't let anyone fool you and talk you into saying you don't need to apply the blood of Jesus.

"Through the Blood of Jesus, I am redeemed out of the hand of the evil one" (Ephesians 1:17).

Romans 5:9 says that I am justified (just as if I'd never done it) through the blood of Jesus Christ.

I grew up being told that I was "stupid" and that I would never amount to anything in life. Words are seeds. Once you speak them out loud, they grow and produce either life or death. These words wreaked havoc over my life until one day, the Lord revealed to me that I needed to break all the word curses that had been spoken over my life since I was a little girl.

On the flip side, as someone in authority, whether you're a parent, teacher, coach, or pastor, exercise caution with the words spoken in moments of anger. Your authority amplifies the impact of your words, and expressions of anger can inadvertently turn into curses. Releasing powerful words in anger toward your child, spouse, or others is like casting a curse. By cursing your own bloodline, you potentially open the gates and grant the enemy access and legal rights to wreak havoc in your life and that of your family.

What about the inner vows you might have made during a traumatic experience? Perhaps you said something like, "I will never be like my mother," or "Never again will I allow anyone to get so close to me to hurt me again." It's time to break these inner vows, as they may be hindering your destiny. Ask God for forgiveness for making those vows. Good news: Once it is brought out into the light, your next steps are:

- Repent for coming into agreement with the lies and the curses. Confess the sins of your forefathers and ancestors (known and unknown). And if you're the one who cursed your child or a spouse in anger, then repent quickly and break the curse.
- Renounce them.
- Denounce them.
- Command every demon associated with the curse to be broken and tell them to leave immediately in the Mighty Name of Jesus.
- Apply the blood over everything that concerns you.
- Renew your covenant with the Lord Jesus!

Indeed, there is nothing stronger than the blood of Jesus. It protects, sanctifies, heals, delivers, cleanses, and provides beyond measure. Covenants are binding agreements between two parties. To break these evil covenants, you require something much stronger. There is nothing more powerful than the blood of Jesus. Apply the blood of Jesus and let heaven and earth bear witness that you are in covenant with Christ alone. Declare that you are loosed from every evil covenant!

> "And you, being dead in your trespasses and the uncircumcision of your flesh, He has made alive together with Him, having forgiven you all trespasses, having wiped out the handwriting of requirements (decrees) that was against us, which was contrary to us. And He has taken it out of the way, having nailed it to the cross. Having disarmed principalities and powers,

He made a public spectacle of them, triumphing over them in it" (Colossians 2:13-15).

A final thought on generational iniquities: One of the prayers I've uttered is inspired by Psalm 142:7: "Bring my soul out of prison that I may praise your name." Asking for deliverance from the prison of my soul, which represents the mind, will, and emotions. Like Joseph thrown into a pit due to the iniquities of his bloodline, some with great callings can find themselves in a metaphorical pit shaped by the iniquities of their bloodline. Joseph found himself in a pit because of the bloodline iniquity of deception.

If you've experienced emotional, health, or financial imprisonment, it's time to declare your freedom. Break free from the prison of shame, fear, and abandonment. Declare this: "I am walking out of this prison into my freedom in the mighty name of Jesus." The doors are open, and the angel of God has come to lead you out. Walk out with your loved ones—children, family, siblings, and spouse. It's time to break free from years of abuse, rejection, emotional wounds, addiction, procrastination, delay, and financial burdens. Step out of the pit and witness Jesus lifting you from the power of the grave. Say goodbye to rejection and double-mindedness. Enough is enough!

Day Three: Seek, Knock, Ask

This is the day we have all been waiting for. We have gotten all the crap out of the way. Now it's time to ASK BIG!

You do not serve a small God. He is the King of all Kings! He sits enthroned above the circle of the earth. The earth is the Lord's and the fullness thereof. He is the one who says, "Behold, I am the Lord of all flesh. Is there anything too hard for Me?" (Jeremiah 32:27).

His hands are not too small, nor are his ears deaf that he cannot hear you. Your prayers are His delight. Ask like your life depends on it because it does. Nations are waiting for you to be delivered, to become who God created you to be so that you can do what he has assigned you to do and accomplish here on earth. It's time to stop thinking small. Get out of your own way, whatever lies you have believed in the past about coming to ask "big."

Lies like "I am not worthy to receive anything good from God." Yes, we are not worthy of anything except that Jesus saw fit to go to the cross and die on our behalf for our sins. And because of the finished work of Christ, we can now come bold into the throne room of God to obtain mercy in our times of need (Hebrews 4:16).

"Therefore, brethren, having boldness to enter the Holiest by the blood of Jesus, by a new and living way which he conse-crated for us, through the veil, that is, His flesh, and having a High Priest over the house of God, let us draw near with a true heart in full assurance of faith, having our hearts sprin-kled from an evil conscience and our bodies washed with pure water" (Hebrews 10:19-22).

Jesus is the answer! His blood has given us access to ask. He said when you ask for bread, He will not give you a stone. If you ask for a fish, He will not give you a snake. So if you are evil, knowing how to give good gifts to your children, how much more will your Father give good things to those who ask him (Matthew 7:9-11, paraphrased).

Write down a list of all the things you have been praying about. Things that have occupied your mind for some time now. You have put that thing to the side because you haven't seen the answers, or perhaps you've given up on the thing or the person. Is it your marriage? Finances? Your children? Your relationships? Your health? Have you recently received bad news from the doctor? It doesn't matter what it is. It's time to ask BIG!

This is why the Bible says: Some things only come out through Prayer and Fasting. Could this be that thing?

It's time to go to war for your breakthrough! It's time to take your position as a son or daughter. Until now, the kingdom of God has suffered violence, and violence takes it by force.

You ask, "How do we take it by force?" I'm glad you asked. You take it by faith. You reclaim what was stolen from you by faith. In Mark 11:24, the word "receive" means "to lay hold of it and not let go," "to claim it," or "to seize it." Receive what God has for you and do not release your grip.

The problem is, most Christians remain passive while awaiting God to act. No, God already performed an incredible deed 2000 years ago when He sent Jesus Christ to hang on that old rugged cross and declared, "It is finished!" Christ died, descended into hell, retrieved the keys, and triumphed victoriously over hell, death, and the grave. He rose on the third day and ascended into heaven, where He sits at the right hand of the Father. He purchased all that pertains to life and godliness and bestowed it upon us, His bride.

We don't need to wait for God to act. All we need to do is remember what He did for us on the cross, understand who we are in Christ, remind ourselves of the Word of God, and reclaim what rightfully belongs to us!

The Holy Spirit could say the same thing to us as He said to Moses, "Why do you cry to Me? Tell the children of Israel to go forward. But lift up your rod, and stretch out your hand over the sea and divide it. And the children of Israel shall go on dry ground through the midst of the sea" (Exodus 14:15-16).

Why do we cry out to God? Take up the rod of faith, the Word of God, and remember who you are in Christ! Take it by faith, by fire, and by force.

Consider the following scriptures:

> *"So Jesus answered and said to them, "Have faith in God. For assuredly, I say to you, whoever says to this mountain, 'Be removed and be cast into the sea,' and does not doubt in his heart, but believes that those things he says will be done, he will have whatever he says. Therefore I say to you, whatever things you ask when you pray, believe that you receive them, and you will have them"*
> *(Mark 11:22-24).*

"And whatever you ask in My name, that I will do,
that the Father may be glorified in the Son. If you ask
anything in My name, I will do it"
(John 14:13-14).

"And in that day you will ask Me nothing. Most assuredly,
I say to you, whatever you ask the Father in My name He
will give you. 24 Until now you have asked nothing in My
name. Ask, and you will receive, that your joy may be full"
(John 16:23-24).

Worship and dance before the king today. As you worship, declare the goodness and the faithfulness of your God. Rest assured that He is watching over His Word to perform it.

Thank Him for answered prayers!

"Now this is the confidence that we have in Him, that if we
ask anything according to His will, He hears us"
(1 John 5:14).

"Now to Him who is able to do exceedingly
abundantly above all that we ask or think, according
to the power that works in us"
(Ephesians 3:20).

"If you abide in Me, and My words abide in you,
you will ask what you desire, and it shall be done for you.
By this My Father is glorified, that you bear much fruit;
so you will be My disciples"
(John 15:7-8).

BECOME THE PERSON WHO CAN DO WHAT IS REQUIRED IN ORDER TO HAVE THOSE THINGS YOU DESIRE

"Then God blessed them, and God said to them,
'Be fruitful and multiply; fill the earth and subdue it;
have dominion over the fish of the sea, over the birds of the
air, and over every living thing that moves on the earth.'"

—Genesis 1:28

I commend you for completing this book. In today's distracted world, finishing what you start is a significant accomplishment. Your dedication to reading this book from cover to cover sets you apart as someone who is truly committed to transforming their life, moving from mediocrity to living purposefully. You aspire to break free from living life by default and are determined to learn, grow, and cultivate your identity as a child of the Most High God.

Now that you've learned these strategies, I hope you'll take action and use them in your life, just as I have in my relationships and business. This book is just the beginning of your journey toward a meaningful relationship with Christ and the Holy Spirit, helping you break free from the mundane and live life by design. This path involves becoming the person you were created to be so that you can accomplish the things you were meant to do in order to have those things you desire to have.

There is one more concept that I believe I need to share with you before we end this book.

The Bible says that Satan, *the thief*, has come to kill, steal, and destroy, but Jesus came so that we may have life and that we may have it more abundantly. At the same token, we have been given authority by Jesus to trample on serpents and scorpions and over all the power of the enemy, and nothing shall by any means hurt us. Clearly, Satan is the enemy, and he is the thief that has come to steal from us.

Paul also reminded us in Romans 8:16-17 that "The Spirit Himself bears witness with our spirit, that we are the children of God. And if children, then heirs—heirs of God and joint heirs with Christ, if indeed we suffer with him, that we may also be glorified together."

We are not just ordinary individuals; we are children of the Most High God and heirs of Christ. Being heirs carries profound significance, signifying our legal entitlement to the property, rank, and legacy of another upon their death. We inherit and continue the legacy of our predecessor, and in our case, we inherit everything that belonged to Jesus after His death. This inheritance includes His power, as stated in Luke 10:19.

On the other hand, the Bible says, "People do not despise a thief if he steals to satisfy himself when he is starving. Yet when he is found, he must restore sevenfold; he may have to give up all the substance of his house" (Proverbs 6:30-31).

Satan, the ultimate thief, seeks to plunder and rob us of our identity, joy, peace, inheritance, finances, relationships, and opportunities. However, God, recognizing us as heirs with Christ, urges us to assert our authority and command Satan to repay what he has stolen. As recipients of Christ's authority, we have the right to demand a sevenfold restitution. This is our position in Christ—a call to exercise our responsibility to rule over Satan in our lives. We are not meant to passively endure his actions; instead, God has empowered us to have dominion over the works of His hand.

"What is man that You are mindful of him, and the son of man, that You visit him? For You made him a little lower than the angels, and You have crowned him with glory and honor. You have made him to have dominion over the works of Your hands; You have put all things under his feet" (Psalm 8:4-6).

In Revelation 1:5-6, we are affirmed as kings and priests unto our God. Through Christ, we have been called to the status of kings in His Kingdom. As kings, we have dominion and the authority to reign. Our responsibility, in this position, is to command Satan to return everything he has stolen from us. It is not just a duty; it is our inheritance. So next time Satan steals something from you, rather than blaming God and looking to Him to get it back for you, by the authority given to you by Christ, command a sevenfold payback!

Finally, in Genesis 1, the very first thing that God showed us about himself is that He is creative. How do I know that? The first thing He told us about ourselves is that He created us in His image. In other words, He created us to be creative. You and I were created by a creative God to be creative. In verse 28 of Genesis chapter 1, it says, "Then God blessed them, and God said to them, 'Be fruitful and multiply; fill the earth and subdue it; have dominion over the fish of the sea, over the birds of the air, and over every living thing that moves on the earth.'"

In other words, He said we are blessed. "Go and be fruitful, multiply, replenish the earth, subdue it, and have dominion!" He blessed us with the ability and the capacity to complete whatever our assignment is right here on planet Earth. I firmly believe that He would not have given you the assignment if He knew you couldn't complete it.

According to 2 Peter 1:3, "His divine power has given to us all things that *pertain* to life and godliness, through the knowledge of Him who called us by glory and virtue." God knows you can, even when you think you can't. When He says "Be" fruitful, it doesn't just mean to have children. No! This also means to be effective, to be capable, to be productive, to be skillful, to grow, to increase. You get my drift.

And then He said to "multiply, fill the earth, and subdue it." God commands us to "Do" these three things to "Have" dominion. To "multiply" in the original Hebrew, according to Strong's Concordance, means "to increase greatly and exceedingly," "to do much in respect of greatly."

To replenish the earth means "to complete, to accomplish." In other words, make it better than you found it. So in order to "Have," we must "Be Doers." And in order to "Do the things," we must "Become the person." We must Become more today than we were yesterday. We must Be like Christ. Jesus cast out demons. When God, His Father, said, "Go," He did not hesitate. He did what His father told Him to do. He taught with authority and power.

Jesus used the Word of God to rebuke the devil when He was tempted. We, too, must do the same. Jesus taught us to take our thoughts captive because He knows the battlefield is in the mind. Everything starts in the mind. Your thoughts start in the mind. Your imagination starts in the mind. And so you become what your thoughts are because "as a man thinks, so is he."

Therefore, Be determined to Become so full of the Word of God that Satan has no room to mess with your mind. Learn how to use truthful words to communicate. Why? "Life and death is in the power of your tongue," my friend! You cannot escape it. Your words are powerful. Your words will make or break you. Your words will shape the trajectory of your life. The Bible is so full of success strategies that, if applied, it can make us Become more than we could ever imagine.

Become a better parent so that you can raise God-fearing, successful adults. Become a better spouse in order to have the kind of hot, sexy marriage you desire to have. Become a better business owner in order to have the power and influence that belongs to riches and wealth.

Joshua 1:8 shows us that everything God has ever created was created for you to become successful. And you are part of God's success plan. Success in your marriage. Success in your relationships. Success in your finances. And success in life! How about that? Imagine overcoming the things holding you back and keeping you stuck. Things like self-doubt, limiting beliefs, lack of confidence, focus, and imposter syndrome.

I firmly believe that one of my life's purposes is to convey that God's Word is full of practical, relevant, and immediate application to whatever challenges you face today. It is the solution to your "Goliath," the means of deliverance from your personal "lion's den," and the path to escape the storms you are encountering right now.

God's Word contains the answers, and when you apply it to your life, you will undoubtedly see and experience the healing, the deliverance, the success, and the blessings.

Lastly, I absolutely love to insert my name inside the scriptures when it's appropriate, of course. This particular passage is one of those times when it is absolutely appropriate to insert your name. Let's take a look together. Joshua 21:45 says, "Not a word failed of any good thing which the LORD had spoken to the house of Israel. All came to pass."

Now, let's add your name. Instead of "the house of Israel," insert your name. For example: Not a word failed of any good thing which the LORD had spoken to the house of Lara. It all came to pass! Be sure to put your name in that scripture, my friend! It is powerful!

My final thought: Are you ready to break barriers and unleash your unstoppable potential? Do you desire to come out of the rut, break off your limitations, and learn the skills needed to succeed widely in every area of your life?

In essence, your main purpose on earth is to know Him, experience the power of His resurrection, and make Him known throughout the world. Your gifts and talents serve as vehicles through which you express and fulfill this purpose. This is our mandate as children of the Most High God. We are called to boldly storm the gates of hell and reclaim what the enemy has stolen from us.

You are destined for greatness, and because of that, the enemy does not want you to realize the magnitude of the power you possess. The truths you have learned in this book will provide divine wisdom on how to govern your family's affairs, strengthen your relationships, and go out to claim territories for the kingdom of God.

You may have been wounded, left battered, broken, and bruised on the sidewalk of life for a season, but it's time to get up, regroup, recharge, and reclaim your position of authority. Your mess is about to be turned into a message, and your brokenness will turn into boldness.

It's time to shift from a lack mindset to an abundance mindset so that you can be empowered to go out there and do those things that you desire and ultimately thrive in a realm where the seemingly impossible becomes possible. Here, you can do what God knew you were capable of doing all along. Are you ready to get unstuck from ALL THE THINGS holding you back and learn to truly step into ALL that you were called TO BE … BOLD AND UNSTOPPABLE? It's time!

I'm on a mission to share my story, empower others for success, and inspire them to turn their trials into triumphs. That's why I've created this brand-new resource just for you.

I would like to invite you to embark on a transformative journey with the S.O.A.R. Success Mastery Course, crafted to unleash your untapped potential and break through barriers. Explore modules like "Setting The Table For Success: Your Unique Value Proposition," designed to furnish you with skills and tools for influencing your world and making a meaningful impact.

Drawing from personal experiences, we help you move from confusion to a clear path of success, building unwavering confidence with practical tools for a fulfilling life, a thriving business, and meaningful relationships. This course is the culmination of my passion to see you WIN and embrace the life God intended. Join me on this incredible journey—explore the S.O.A.R. Success Mastery Course and confidently step into your bright future.

In this course, we'll provide the necessary tools for you to become all you were meant to be. Resolve to ensure that the rest of your life is the best part of your life. Learn how to become more so that you can do the things you are called to do and impact many lives.

This course is designed to help you overcome excuses, achieve financial success, enhance relationships, and thrive in every aspect of life. Our goal is to empower you to advance the kingdom of God right here on earth by taking dominion over your area of assignment.

Visit www.laratugbiyele.com/soarsuccess to get on the waitlist and be notified when the course is released.

Remember, God has incredible plans for you! You were intricately designed by a creative Father, and that same creativity resides within you. Now is the time to discover how to use your God-given talents, gifts, and passions to lead a successful life that impacts the world around you and honors God. Let it be said of you that none of the good promises the Lord made to your house failed; everything came to pass. Everything!

I'll see you in the course.

ACKNOWLEDGMENTS

Wow! It feels surreal to be writing these words for my completed book. First and foremost, I want to express my heartfelt gratitude to my Abba Father! Thank you, Jesus, for being my rock and walking with me all these years. If it had not been for Jesus, where would I be? I am grateful for the truth of your Word because it has led me to where I am today.

To the most supportive husband anyone could have asked for—Foley! Thank you for all your encouragement and the push to find my voice and get it in writing. I love you so much!

To my three beautiful children, you are like arrows in the hand of a warrior. You are the best children a mom could ever ask for. Thank you for being supportive and always cheering me on.

To my mom, for all the years of sacrifices you made for all six of your children. Thank you for being a good mom. I love you.

To all my friends and families who have encouraged me along the way. Thank you for your prayers.

ABOUT THE AUTHOR

Lara Tugbiyele is a dynamic speaker, transformation coach, and a source of inspiration for those seeking to overcome adversity and find their path to success. She has played a pivotal role in helping people facing challenges in different areas of life to break free from the feeling of being "stuck."

By identifying and reversing the patterns of a mindset programmed for failure in their minds, Lara has empowered individuals to S.O.A.R. beyond adversity, master their mindset, multiply their money, and mend their meaningful relationships.

Her journey, rooted in personal experiences of growing up in a challenging environment characterized by rejection, abuse, and poverty, has equipped her with the wisdom of resilience, forgiveness, and unwavering faith. Her transformation from a state of despair to a position of authority stands as a testament to the life-changing influence of God's power, as well as the strategies she shares in this book.

Driven by a deep desire to help others realize their full potential, Lara has emerged as an engaging coach for those who seek to find their life's purpose, cultivate strong relationships, and attain financial prosperity.

Lara lives in Georgia with her husband, three children, and their mini Goldendoodle.

www.ingramcontent.com/pod-product-compliance
Lightning Source LLC
Chambersburg PA
CBHW060434130626
46555CB00005B/2356